To Hazel,

I know how much you
like animals - so thought
you would like this
book!

    Love from
        Beena
            x

December 2007

1000 FACTS ON
ANIMALS

First published by Bardfield Press in 2005
Copyright © 2001 Miles Kelly Publishing Ltd

Bardfield Press is an imprint of
Miles Kelly Publishing Ltd,
Bardfield Centre, Great Bardfield, Essex, CM7 4SL

Some material in this book appears in the *1000 Things You Should Know* series

4 6 8 10 9 7 5 3

Editor
Belinda Gallagher

Assistant Editor
Mark Darling

Art Director
Clare Sleven

Designer
Debbie Meekcoms

Picture Researcher
Liberty Newton

British Library Cataloguing-in-Publication Data
A catalogue record for this book is available from the British Library

ISBN 1-84236-027-2

Printed in China

www.mileskelly.net
info@mileskelly.net

1000 FACTS ON
ANIMALS

John Farndon
Consultant Steve Parker

BARDFIELD
PRESS

Contents

Key

 Insects, spiders and creepy crawlies

 Sea creatures

 Reptiles and amphibians

 Birds

 Mammals

How animals live

Contents

Contents

What are insects?

◄ Insects were the first creatures to live on land – nearly a quarter of a billion years before the first dinosaurs – and the first to fly.

● **Insects** may be tiny, but there are more of them than all the other animals put together – over 1 million known species.

● **They range** from tiny flies to huge beetles, and they are found everywhere there is land.

● **Insects** have six legs and a body divided into three sections – which is why they are called insects ('in sections'). The sections are the head, thorax (middle) and abdomen.

● **An insect's body** is encased in such a tough shell (its exoskeleton) that there is no need for bones.

● **Insects grow** by getting rid of their old exoskeleton and replacing it with a bigger one. This is called moulting.

● **Insects change** dramatically as they grow. Butterflies, moths, and beetles undergo metamorphosis (see butterflies). Grasshoppers and mayflies begin as wingless nymphs, then gradually grow wings with each moult. Silverfish and springtails simply get bigger with each moult.

● **Insects' eyes** are called compound because they are made up of many lenses – from six (worker ants) to more than 30,000 (dragonflies).

● **Insects have** two antennae (feelers) on their heads.

- **Insects** do not have lungs. Instead, they breathe through holes in their sides called spiracles, linked to their body through tubes called tracheae.

- **The world's longest insect** is the giant stick insect of Indonesia, which can grow to 33 cm long.

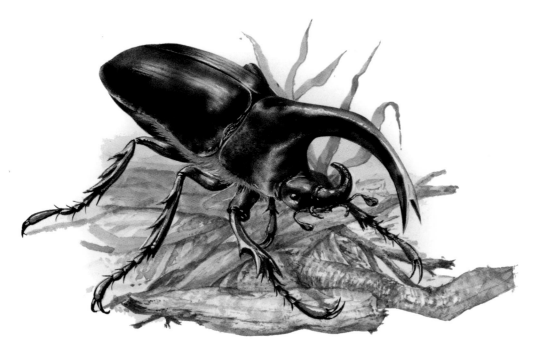

▲ *The rhinoceros beetle shown here can push an object 850 times its own weight, which is equivalent to a person pushing a 50-tonne army tank!*

Worms

- **Worms** are long, wriggling, tube-like animals. Annelids are worms such as the earthworm whose bodies are divided into segments.

- **There are 15,000 species** of annelid. Most live underground in tunnels, or in the sea.

- **The world's largest earthworm** is the giant earthworm of South Africa, which can grow to as long as 6.5 m when fully extended.

- **Earthworms** spend their lives burrowing through soil. Soil goes in the mouth end, passes through the gut and comes out at the tail end.

- **An earthworm** is both male and female (hermaphrodite), and after two earthworms mate, both develop eggs.

- **Over half the annelid species** are marine (sea) bristleworms, such as ragworms and lugworms. They are named because they are covered in bristles, which they use to paddle over the seabed or dig into the mud.

▼ *Plants would not grow half as well without earthworms to aerate the soil as they burrow in it, mix up the layers and make it more fertile with their droppings.*

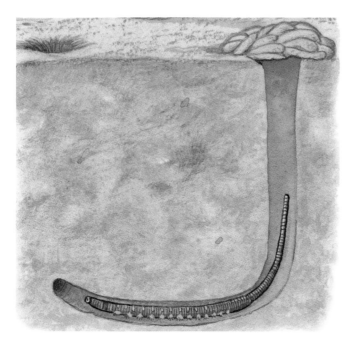

◄ *A lugworm in its U-shaped burrow in the sand. It will stay in its burrow and swallow sand along with bits of dead animal and plant matter. It passes the sand through its body producing a cast – these can be seen on beaches at low tide.*

- **The sea mouse** is a mouse-shaped bristleworm with furry hairs.

- **Flatworms** look like ribbons or as though an annelid worm has been ironed flat. Their bodies donot have proper segments. Of the thousands of flatworm species, many live in the sea or in pond algae.

- **Flukes** are flatworms that live as parasites inside other animals. Diseases like bilharzia are caused by flukes.

- **Tapeworms** are parasitic flatworms that live inside their host's gut and eat their food.

11

Snails and slugs

- **Snails and slugs** are small, squidgy, slimy, soft-bodied crawling creatures. They belong to a huge group of animals called molluscs which have no skeleton. Squid and oysters are also molluscs.

- **Snails and slugs** are gastropods, a group that also includes whelks and winkles.

- **Gastropod** means 'stomach foot', because these animals seem to slide along on their stomachs.

- **Most gastropods** live in the sea. They include limpets which stick firmly to seashore rocks.

- **Most land snails and slugs** ooze a trail of sticky slime to help them move along the ground.

- **Garden snails** are often hermaphrodites, which means they have both male and female sex organs.

▼ *Most slugs, like this great black slug, eat decaying vegetation. Some slugs like the underground parts of plants and young leaves which make them unpopular with gardeners.*

- **The great grey slugs** of western Europe court by circling each other for over an hour on a branch, then launching themselves into the air to hang from a long trail of mucus. They then mate for between 7 to 24 hours.

- **Among the largest gastropods** are the tropical tritons, whose 45–cm shells are sometimes used as warhorns. Conches are another big kind of gastropod.

- **Some cone snails** in the Pacific and Indian oceans have teeth that can inject a poison which can actually kill people.

▶ *Garden snails have a shell which they seal themselves into in dry weather, making a kind of trapdoor to save moisture. They have eyes on their horns.*

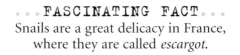

. . . FASCINATING FACT . . .
Snails are a great delicacy in France, where they are called *escargot*.

Beetles

- **At least 250,000** species of beetle have been identified. They live everywhere on Earth, apart from in the oceans.

- **Unlike other insects**, adult beetles have a pair of thick, hard, front wings called elytra. These form an armour-like casing over the beetle's body.

- **The goliath beetle** of Africa is the heaviest flying insect, weighing over 100 grams and growing to as much as 13 cm long.

- **Dung beetles** roll away the dung of grazing animals to lay their eggs on. Fresh dung from one elephant may contain 7,000 beetles – they will clear the dung away in little more than a day.

▶ *The over-sized mandibles (jaws) of these stag beetles are quite harmless. They show that the males have reached maturity and are ready to breed.*

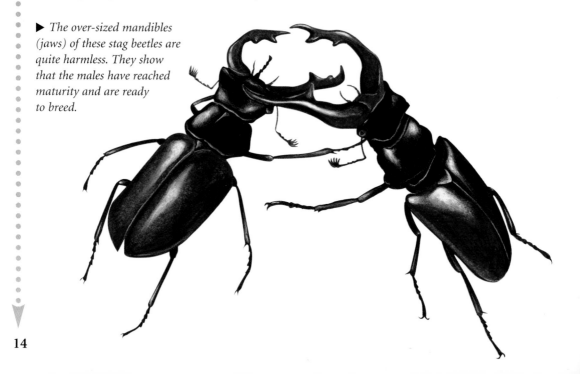

- **A click beetle** can jump 30 cm into the air.

- **The bombardier beetle** shoots attackers with jets of burning chemicals from the tip of its abdomen.

- **The rove beetle** can zoom across water on a liquid given off by glands on its abdomen.

- **The leaf-eating beetle** can clamp on to leaves using the suction of a layer of oil.

- **Stag beetles** have huge jaws which look like a stag's antlers.

Elytra (hard front wings)

▶ *The jewel beetles of tropical South America get their name from the brilliant rainbow colours of their elytra (front wings).*

...FASCINATING FACT...
The Arctic beetle can survive in temperatures below -60°C.

15

Butterflies

- **Butterflies** are insects with four large wings that feed either on the nectar of flowers or on fruit.

- **Together with moths,** butterflies make up the scientific order Lepidoptera – the word means 'scaly wings'. There are more than 165,000 species of Lepidoptera – 20,000 butterflies and 145,000 moths.

▲ *Every species of butterfly has its own wing pattern, just like humans have their own fingerprint.*

- **Many butterflies** are brightly coloured and fly by day. They have slim, hairless bodies and club-shaped antennae (feelers).

- **The biggest butterfly** is the Queen Alexandra's birdwing of New Guinea, with 25 cm-wide wings. The smallest is the Western pygmy blue.

- **Butterflies can only fly** if their wing muscles are warm. To warm up, they bask in the sun so their wings soak up energy like solar panels.

- **The monarch butterfly** is such a strong flier it can cross the Atlantic Ocean (see migration).

- **The shimmering blue wings** of the South American morpho butterfly are very beautiful – in the 19th century millions of the butterflies were caught and made into brooches.

- **Most female butterflies** live only a few days, so they have to mate and lay eggs quickly. Most males court them with elaborate flying displays.

- **Butterflies** taste with their tarsi (feet). Females 'stamp' on leaves to see if they are ripe enough for egg laying.

- **Every butterfly's caterpillar** has its own chosen food plants – different from the flowers the adult feeds on.

1. Egg – eggs are laid on plants that will provide food when the caterpillars hatch

2. Larva – when the caterpillar hatches, it begins eating and growing straight away

3. Pupa – butterfly caterpillars develop hard cases and hang from a stem or leaf

5. Imago – the adult's new wings are damp and crumpled, but soon dry in the sun

4. Metamorphosis – it takes a few days to a year for the pupa to turn into an adult

▶ Few insects change as much as butterflies do during their lives. Butterflies start off as an egg, then hatch into a long, wiggly larva called a caterpillar, which eats leaves greedily and grows rapidly. When it is big enough, the caterpillar makes itself a case, which can be either a cocoon or a chrysalis. Inside, it metamorphoses (changes) into an adult, then breaks out, dries its new wings and flies away.

... FASCINATING FACT ...
Butterflies fly like no other insects, flapping their wings like birds.

17

Moths

- **Like butterflies,** moths belong to the insect group Lepidoptera.

- **Most moths** have fat, hairy bodies, and feathery or thread-like antennae.

- **Many moths** fly at dusk or at night. By day, they rest on tree trunks and in leaf litter, where their drab colour makes them hard for predators such as birds to spot. However, there are also many brightly coloured day-flying moths.

- **Tiger moths** give out high-pitched clicks to warn that they taste bad and so escape being eaten.

- **The biggest moths** are the Hercules moth and the bent wing ghost moth of Asia, with wingspans of over 25 cm.

- **Night-flying** moths shiver their wings to warm them up for flight.

▲ *Among the world's largest moths, moon moths are named after their moon-like wing markings. The male's feathery antennae can pick up the scent of a female from 2-3 km away.*

- **Hawk moths** are powerful fliers and migrate long distances. The oleander hawk moth flies from tropical Africa to far northern Europe in summer.

- **The caterpillars of small moths** live in seeds, fruit, stems and leaves, eating them from the inside.

- **The caterpillars of big moths** feed on leaves from the outside, chewing chunks out of them.

▲ *Hawk moths have very long tongues for sucking nectar from flowers. They often hover like hummingbirds as they are feeding.*

- **When threatened,** the caterpillar of the puss moth rears up and thrusts its whip-like tail forward, and squirts a jet of formic acid from its head end.

- **Every caterpillar spins silk,** but the cloth silk comes from the caterpillar of the white Bombyx mori moth, known as the silkworm.

19

Bees and wasps

- **Bees and wasps** are narrow-waisted insects (usually with hairy bodies). Many suck nectar from flowers.

- **There are 22,000 species of bee.** Some, like leaf-cutter bees, live alone. But most, like honey bees and bumble bees, live in vast colonies.

- **Honey bees** live in hives, either in hollow trees or in man-made beehive boxes. The inside of the hive is a honeycomb made up of hundreds of six-sided cells.

- **A honey bee colony** has a queen (the female bee that lays the eggs), tens of thousands of female worker bees, and a few hundred male drones.

- **Worker bees** collect nectar and pollen from flowers.

- **Each worker bee** makes ten trips a day and visits 1,000 flowers each trip. It takes 65,000 trips to 65 million flowers to make 1 kg of honey.

- **Honey bees** tell others where to find flowers rich in pollen or nectar by flying in a special dance-like pattern.

- **Wasps** do not make honey, but feed on nectar, fruit juice or tiny creatures. Many species have a nasty sting in their tail.

- **Paper wasps build** huge papier maché nests the size of footballs, containing 15,000 or more cells.

- **Paper wasps make** papier maché for their nest by chewing wood and mixing it with their spit.

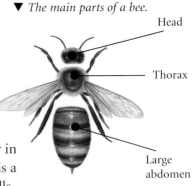

▼ *The main parts of a bee.*

Head

Thorax

Large abdomen

▶ *Honey bees and bumble bees feed on pollen. They make honey from flower nectar to feed their young.*

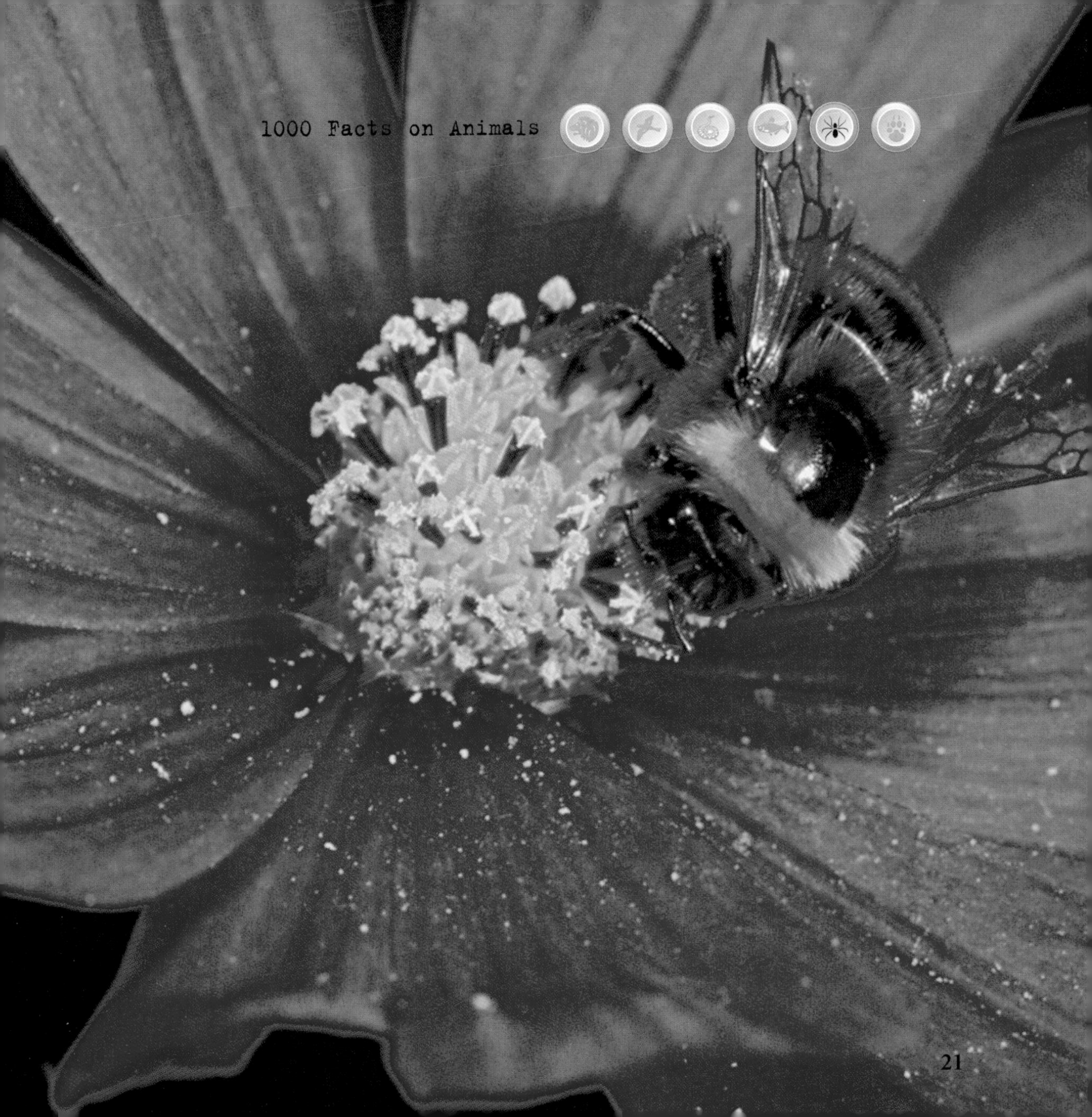

Ants and termites

- Ants are a vast group of insects related to bees and wasps. Most ants have a tiny waist and are wingless.

- Ants are the main insects in tropical forests, living in colonies of anything from 20 to millions.

- Ant colonies are all female. Most species have one or several queens which lay the eggs. Hundreds of soldier ants guard the queen, while smaller workers build the nest and care for the young.

- Males only enter the nest to mate with young queens, then die.

- Wood ants squirt acid from their abdomen to kill enemies.

- Army ants march in huge swarms, eating most small creatures they meet.

- Groups of army ants cut any large prey they catch into pieces which they carry back to the nest. Army ants can carry 50 times their own weight.

- Ants known as slavemakers raid the nests of other ants and steal their young to raise as slaves.

- Termite colonies are even more complex than ant ones. They have a large king and queen who mate, as well as soldiers to guard them and workers to do all the work.

- Termite nests are mounds built like cities with many chambers – including a garden used for growing fungus. Many are air-conditioned with special chimneys.

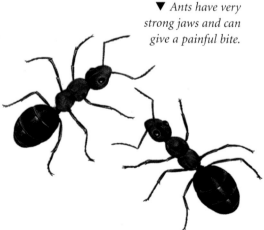

▼ *Ants have very strong jaws and can give a painful bite.*

▶ *African termites use mud and saliva to build amazing nests more than 12 m high, housing over 5 million termites. Termites* (Isoptera) *belong to a separate insect group from ants, bees and wasps* (Hymenoptera).

23

Flies

▶ *Flies have only one pair of proper wings. The hind wings are small stumps called halteres which help a fly balance in flight.*

- **Flies** are one of the biggest groups of insects, common nearly everywhere – there are over 90,000 species.

- **Unlike other insects,** flies have only one pair of proper wings.

- **Flies** include bluebottles, black flies, gnats, horseflies, midges, mosquitoes and tsetse flies.

- **A house fly** flies at over 7 km/h – equal to flying 350,000 times its own length in an hour. If a jumbo jet flew at the same speed relative to its length for an hour, it would get almost right around the world.

- **Alaskan flies** can stand being frozen at temperatures of -60°C and still survive.

▶ *Mosquitoes can spread dangerous diseases and their bite is painful. They have a sharp tube (proboscis) with which they pierce their victim's skin. Saliva then mixes with the blood to prevent it clotting.*

- **Flies suck up** their food – typically sap from rotting plants and fruit. Houseflies often suck liquids from manure. Blowflies drink from rotting meat.

- **The larvae (young) of flies** are called maggots, and they are tiny, white, wriggling tube-shapes.

- **Flies resemble or mimic** many other kinds of insects. There are wasp flies, beetle flies, ant flies and moth flies.

- **Many species** of fly are carriers of dangerous diseases. When a fly bites or makes contact, it can infect people with some of the germs it carries – especially the flies that suck blood. Mosquitoes spread malaria, and tsetse flies spread sleeping sickness.

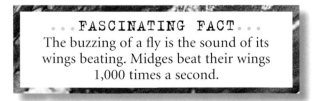

.**.FASCINATING FACT**...
The buzzing of a fly is the sound of its wings beating. Midges beat their wings 1,000 times a second.

Dragonflies

- **Dragonflies** are big hunting insects with four large transparent wings, and a long slender body that may be a shimmering red, green or blue.

- **Dragonflies have** 30,000 separate lenses in each of their compound eyes, giving them the sharpest vision of any insect.

- **A dragonfly** can see something that is stationary from almost 2 m away, and something moving two to three times farther away.

- **As it swoops** in on its prey, a dragonfly pulls its legs forwards like a basket to scoop up its victim.

- **Dragonflies** often mate in mid-air, and the male may then stay hanging on to the female until she lays her eggs.

  - **Dragonfly eggs** are laid in water or in the stem of a water plant, and hatch in 2 to 3 weeks.

    - **Newly-hatched dragonflies** are called nymphs and look like fatter, wingless adults.

      - **Dragonfly nymphs** are ferocious hunters, often feeding on young fish and tadpoles.

        - **Dragonfly nymphs** grow and moult over a period of several years before they climb on to a reed or rock to emerge as an adult.

◄ *Dragonflies are big insects even today, but hundreds of millions of years ago, there were dragonflies with wings that were well over 70 cm across.*

▲ *A blue dragonfly rests on a flower. A stream or pond is sure to be nearby.*

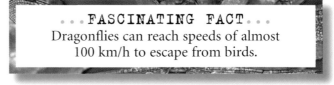

...FASCINATING FACT...
Dragonflies can reach speeds of almost
100 km/h to escape from birds.

Grasshoppers and crickets

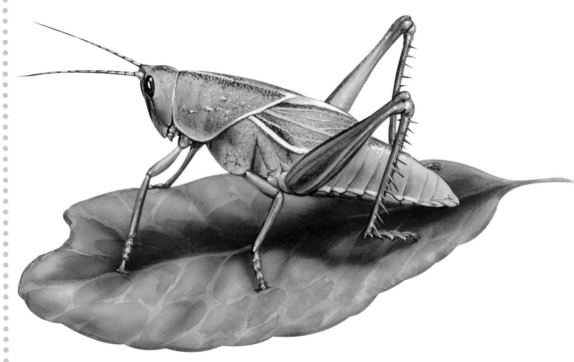

▲ *The spikes on the long-horned grasshopper's back legs are what make the chirruping sound as it rubs them against its forewings.*

- **Grasshoppers** are plant-eating insects related to crickets, locusts and katydids.

- **Grasshoppers** belong to two main families – short-horned, which includes locusts, and long-horned, which includes katydidsand crickets.

▶ *The mole cricket digs out its tunnel home where it rests and feeds. The male's burrow has a tapering shape like a megaphone to louden his mating chirrup.*

- **Short-horned grasshoppers** have ears on the side of their body. Long-horned grasshoppers have ears in their knees.

- **Grasshoppers** have powerful back legs, which allow them to jump huge distances.

- Some **grasshoppers** can leap more than 3 m.

- **Grasshoppers** sing by rubbing their hind legs across their closed forewings.

- **A grasshopper's singing** is called stridulation.

- **Crickets** chirrup faster the warmer it is.

- **If you count** the number of chirrups a snowy tree cricket gives in 15 seconds, then add 40, you get the temperature in degrees Fahrenheit.

. . . **FASCINATING FACT** . . .
A frightened lubber grasshopper oozes a
horrible-smelling froth from its mouth.

Fleas and lice

- **Fleas and lice** are small wingless insects that live on birds and mammals, including humans. Dogs, cats and rats are especially prone to fleas.

- **Fleas and sucking lice** suck their host's blood.

- **Chewing lice** chew on their host's skin and hair or feathers. Chewing lice do not live on humans.

▼ *The human head louse has a body length of 2-3mm. Once its crab-like legs and hooked claws cling to its victim's hair or skin, it is harder to shift than a limpet on a seaside rock.*

- **Fleas and lice** are often too small to see easily. But adult fleas grow to over 2 mm long.

- **A flea** can jump 30 cm in the air – the equivalent of a human leaping 200 m in the air.

- **The fleas** in flea circuses perform tricks such as jumping through hoops and pulling wagons.

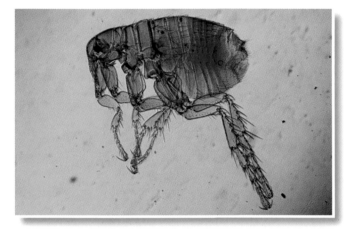

▲ *A much-magnified flea with its powerful back legs for jumping.*

- **Fleas spread** by jumping from one animal to another, to suck their blood.

- **When fleas lay their eggs,** they hatch as larvae and crawl off into the host's bedding, where they spin cocoons and emerge as adults 2 weeks later.

- **Head lice** gum their nits (eggs) to hair and spread from head to head through sharing of combs and hats.

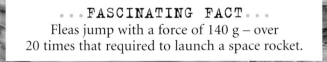

...FASCINATING FACT...
Fleas jump with a force of 140 g – over
20 times that required to launch a space rocket.

Poisonous insects

◄ The bold colouring of the ladybird warns birds that it is not for eating. It has a healthy appetite for aphids making it every gardener's friend.

● **Insects are small,** but many have nasty poisons to protect themselves.

● **Most poisonous insects** are brightly coloured – including many caterpillars, wasps and cardinal beetles – to warn off potential enemies.

● **Ants, bees and wasps** have stings in their tails which they use to inject poison to defend themselves or paralyse prey.

● **Bee and wasp stings** have barbed ends to keep the sting in long enough to inject the poison. Honey bees cannot pull the barb out from human skins, and so tear themselves away and die.

► The hornet is really a large wasp. Its brightly striped body is a warning to others animals that it stings. When the hornet does sting, it injects a venom that causes a painful swelling.

- **Velvet ants** are not really ants at all, but wingless wasps with such a nasty sting that they are called 'cow killers'.

- **Ladybirds** make nasty chemicals in their knees.

- **When attacked,** swallowtail caterpillars whip out a smelly forked gland from a pocket behind their head and hit their attacker with it.

- **The lubber grasshopper** is slow moving, but when attacked it oozes a foul-smelling froth from its mouth and thorax.

- **The bombardier beetle** squirts out a spray of liquid from its rear end, almost like a small spray-gun! This startles and stings the attacker and gives the small beetle time to escape.

▲ *The caterpillar of a swallowtail butterfly. Most swallowtails are tropical.*

Spiders

▶ *Like all arachnids, spiders have eight legs, plus two 'arms' called pedipalps and a pair of fangs called chelicerae. They also have eight simple eyes.*

- **Spiders** are small scurrying creatures which, unlike insects, have eight legs not six, and bodies with two parts not three.

- **Spiders** belong to a group of 70,000 creatures called arachnids, which also includes scorpions, mites and ticks.

- **Spiders** live in nooks and crannies almost everywhere in the world, especially where there is plenty of vegetation to feed tiny creatures.

- **Spiders are hunters** and most of them feed mainly on insects. Despite their name, bird-eating spiders rarely eat birds, preferring lizards and small rodents such as mice.

- **Spiders have eight eyes,** but most have poor eyesight and hunt by feeling vibrations with their legs.

- **Many spiders** catch their prey by weaving silken nets called webs. Some webs are simple tubes in holes. Others, called orb webs, are elaborate and round. Spiders' webs are sticky to trap insects.

- **The Australian trapdoor** spider ambushes its prey from a burrow with a camouflaged entrance flap.

- **Most spiders** have a poisonous bite which they use to stun or kill their prey. Tarantulas and sun spiders crush their victims with their powerful jaws.

- **The bite of black widow** and red-back funnel-web spiders is so poisonous that it can kill humans.

▶ *All spiders produce silk. Some turn this silk into inticate webs, first for catching prey and then for trussing them up.*

...**FASCINATING FACT**...
Female black widow spiders eat their mates after mating.

35

What is a fish?

- **Fish** are mostly slim, streamlined animals that live in water. Many are covered in tiny shiny plates called scales. Most have bony skeletons and a backbone.

- **There are well over 21,000 species** of fish, ranging from the 8 mm-long pygmy goby to the 12 m-long whale shark.

- **Fish** are cold-blooded.

- **Fish breathe** through gills – rows of feathery brushes inside each side of the fish's head.

- **To get oxygen**, fish gulp water in through their mouths and draw it over their gills.

- **Fish** have fins for swimming, not limbs.

- **Most fish** have a pectoral fin behind each gill and two pelvic fins below to the rear, as well as a dorsal fin on top of their body, an anal fin beneath, and a caudal (tail) fin.

- **Fish let gas in** and out of their swim bladders to float at particular depths.

- **Some fish** communicate by making sounds with their swim bladder. Catfish use them like bagpipes.

▲ *The arapaima lives in the swampy parts of tropical south America. It can breathe in the normal fish way using its gills or gulp down air. It can grow to a vast 3 m in length and weigh up to 200 kg.*

▼ *Angling (catching fish) is a popular pastime all around the world. The fish is hooked as it bites the lure or bait.*

...FASCINATING FACT...
The drum fish makes a drumming sound
with its swim bladder.

37

Jellyfish

- **Jellyfish** are sea creatures with bell-shaped, jelly-like bodies, and long stinging tentacles.

- **Biologists** call jellyfish medusa, after the mythical Greek goddess Medusa, who had wriggling snakes for hair.

- **Jellyfish** belong to a large group of sea creatures called cnidarians, which also includes corals and anemones.

- **Unlike anemones**, jellyfish float about freely, moving by squeezing water out from beneath their body. When a jellyfish stops squeezing, it slowly sinks.

- **A jellyfish's tentacles** are covered with stinging cells called nematocysts, which are used to catch fish and for protection. The stinging cells explode when touched, driving tiny poisonous threads into the victim.

- **Jellyfish vary in size** from a few millimetres to over 2 m.

- **The bell of one giant jellyfish** measured 2.29 m across. Its tentacles were over 36 m long.

- **The Portuguese man-of-war** is not a true jellyfish, but a collection of hundreds of tiny animals called polyps which live together under a gas-filled float.

- **The purple jellyfish** can be red, yellow or purple.

▼ *Jellyfish are among the world's most ancient animals.*

...FASCINATING FACT...
The box jellyfish has one of the deadliest poisons. It can kill a human in 30 seconds.

39

Corals and anemones

▼ *Sea anemones look like flowers with petals, but they are actually carnivorous animals with their ring of tentacles.*

- **Sea anemones** are tiny, meat-eating animals that look a bit like flowers. They cling to rocks and catch tiny prey with their tentacles (see life on the seashore).

- **Coral reefs** are the undersea equivalent of rainforests, teeming with fish and other sea life. The reefs are built by tiny, sea-anemone-like animals called polyps.

▶ *Coral polyps feed mainly on the tiny larvae of sea creatures such as shell fish, which they catch with their tentacles.*

- **Coral polyps** live all their lives in just one place, either fixed to a rock or to dead polyps.

- **When coral polyps die,** their cup-shaped skeletons become hard coral.

- **Coral reefs** are long ridges, mounds, towers and other shapes made from billions of coral polyps and their skeletons.

- **Fringing reefs** are shallow coral reefs that stretch out from the seashore.

- **Barrier reefs** form a long, underwater wall a little way offshore.

- **The Great Barrier Reef** off eastern Australia is the longest reef in the world, stretching over 2,000 km.

- **Coral atolls** are ring-shaped islands that formed from fringing reefs around an old volcano (which has long since sunk beneath the waves).

- **Coral reefs** take millions of years to form – the Great Barrier Reef is 18 million years old, for example. By drilling a core into ancient corals, and analysing the minerals and growth rate, scientists can read history back for millions of years.

Cockles and mussels

▲ *There are two main kinds of seashell – univalves like these (which are a single shell), and bivalves (which come in two, hinged halves).*

- **Cockles and mussels** belong to a group of molluscs called bivalves, which includes oysters, clams, scallops and razorshells.

- **Bivalve** means 'having two valves', and all these creatures have two halves to their shells, joined by a hinge that opens rather like that of a locket.

- **Most bivalves feed** by filtering food out from the water through a tube called a siphon.

- **Cockles** burrow in sand and mud on the seashore. Mussels cling to rocks and breakwaters between the high and low tide marks.

- **Oysters** and some other molluscs line their shells with a hard, shiny, silvery white substance called nacre.

- **When a lump of grit** gets into an oyster shell, it is gradually covered in a ball of nacre, making a pearl.

- **The best pearls** come from the Pinctada pearl oysters that live in the Pacific Ocean. The world's biggest pearl was 12 cm across and weighed 6.4 kg. It came from a giant clam.

- **Scallops** can swim away from danger by opening and shutting their shells rapidly to pump out water. But most bivalves escape danger by shutting themselves up inside their shells.

- **A giant clam** found on the Great Barrier Reef was over 1 m across and weighed more than 0.25 tonnes.

- **There are colonies** of giant clams living many thousands of metres down under the oceans, near hot volcanic vents.

▼ *The swan mussel is a bivalve – a mollusc type of shellfish similar to clams and oysters on the seashore. It lives in lakes and slow, deep rivers. It draws a currrent of water into its shell, both for breathing and to filter out tiny particles of food.*

43

Octopuses and squid

- **Octopuses and squid** belong to a family of molluscs called cephalopods.

- **Octopuses** are sea creatures with a round, soft, boneless body, three hearts and eight long arms called tentacles.

- **An octopus's tentacles** are covered with suckers that allow it to grip rocks and prey.

- **Octopuses** have two large eyes, similar to humans, and a beak-like mouth.

- **When in danger** an octopus may send out a cloud of inky black fluid. Sometimes the ink cloud is the same shape as the octopus and may fool a predator into chasing the cloud.

▶ *Most of the hundreds of species of octopus live on the beds of shallow seas around the world. Octopuses are quite intelligent creatures.*

▶ *The giant squid is rarely seen and s usually partly-decomposed when caught. For this reason it is the subject of many myths. Its eyes however are truly massive, the biggest of any animal.*

- **Some octopuses can change colour** dramatically to startle a predator or blend in with its background.
- **The smallest octopus** is just 2.5 cm across. The biggest measures 6 m from tentacle tip to tentacle tip.
- **A squid** has eight arms and two tentacles and swims by forcing a jet of water out of its body.
- **Giant squid** in the Pacific can grow to 18 m or more long.

. . . **FASCINATING FACT**. . .
The 30 cm-long blue-ringed octopus's poison is so deadly that it kills more people than sharks.

45

Starfish and sea urchins

▲ *Starfish that live in cooler water tend to be brown or yellow, whereas many tropical starfish can be bright red or even blue.*

● **Despite their name** starfish are not fish, but belong instead to a group of small sea creatures called echinoderms.

● **Sea urchins** and sea cucumbers are also echinoderms.

● **Starfish** have star-shaped bodies and are predators that prey mostly on shellfish such as scallops and oysters. They have five, strong arms which they use to prise open their victim. The starfish then inserts its stomach into its victim and sucks out its flesh.

- **Under the arms** of a starfish are hundreds of tiny, tube-like 'feet'. Bigger tubes inside the starfish's body pump water in and out of the 'feet', flexing the arms and driving the starfish along.

- **Starfish** often drop some of their arms off to escape an enemy, but the arms eventually grow again.

- **Sea urchins** are ball-shaped creatures. Their shell is covered with bristling spines, which can be poisonous and can be up to 40 cm long in some species.

- **A sea urchin's spines** are used for protection. Urchins also have sucker-like feet for moving.

- **A sea urchin's mouth** is a hole with five teeth, on the underside of its body.

▲ *Related to sea urchins there are over 1600 species of starfish. They range from less than 1 cm across to over 1 m.*

- **Sea cucumbers** have no shell, but a leathery skin and a covering of chalky plates called spicules.

- **When threatened,** a sea cucumber chucks out pieces of its gut as a decoy and swims away. It grows a new one later.

Crabs and lobsters

- **Crabs and lobsters** are part of an enormous group of creatures called crustaceans.

- **Most crabs and lobsters** have their own shell, but hermit crabs live inside the discarded shells of other creatures.

- **Crabs and lobsters are decapods,** which means they have ten legs – although the first pair are often strong pincers which are used to hold and tear food.

- **For spotting prey**, crabs and lobsters have two pairs of antennae on their heads and a pair of eyes on stalks.

- **One of a lobster's claws** usually has blunt knobs for crushing victims. The other has sharp teeth for cutting.

- **Male fiddler crabs** have one giant pincer which they waggle to attract a mate.

- **Robber crabs** have claws on their legs which they use to climb up trees to escape from predators.

▶ *Lobsters are dark green or blue when alive and only turn red when cooked.*

▲ *Apart from climbing trees the robber crab is notable for another strange and unfortunate characteristic – it drowns in water!*

- **The giant Japanese spider crab** can grow to measure 3 m across between the tips of its outstretched pincers.

- **When American spiny lobsters** migrate, they cling to each others' tails in a long line, marching for hundreds of kilometres along the seabed.

- **Sponge crabs** hide under sponges which they cut to fit. The sponge then grows at the same rate as the crab and keepsit covered.

49

Sharks

- **Sharks** are the most fearsome predatory fish of the seas. There are 375 species, living mostly in warm seas.

- **Sharks** have a skeleton made of rubbery cartilage – most other kinds of fish have bony skeletons.

- **The world's biggest fish** is the whale shark, which can grow to well over 12 m long. Unlike other sharks, the whale shark and the basking shark (at 9 m long) mostly eat plankton and are completely harmless.

- **A shark's main weapons** are its teeth – they are powerful enough to bite through plate steel.

▼ A shark's torpedo-shaped body makes it a very fast swimmer.

- **Sharks** put so much strain on their teeth that they always have three or four spare rows of teeth in reserve.
- **Nurse sharks** grow a new set of teeth every 8 days.
- **Up to 20** people die from recorded shark attacks each year.
- **The killing machine** of the shark world is the great white shark, responsible for most attacks on humans.
- **Hammerhead sharks** can also be dangerous . They have T-shaped heads, with eyes and nostrils at the end of the T.

▶ *The super-streamlined blue shark lives in warm seas and is 3.7 m in length. It has very long side fins and eats surface fish like herring and mackerel.*

. . . . FASCINATING FACT . . .
Great white sharks are the biggest meat-eating
sharks, growing to over 7 m long.

Rays

● **Rays** are a huge group of over 300 species of fish, which includes skates, stingrays, electric rays, manta rays, eagle rays and guitar fish.

● **Many rays** have flat, almost diamond-shaped bodies, with pectoral fins elongated into broad wings. Guitar fish have longer, more shark-like bodies.

● **A ray's gills** are slot-like openings beneath its fins.

● **Rays have no bones.** Instead, like sharks, they are cartilaginous fish – their body framework is made of rubbery cartilage (you have this in your nose and ears).

● **Rays live mostly** on the ocean floor, feeding on seabed creatures such as oysters, clams and other shellfish.

▲ *The Atlantic manta ray is shown here with the much smaller spotted eagle ray.*

- **Manta rays** live near the surface and feed on plankton.
- **The Atlantic manta ray** is the biggest ray, often over 7 m wide and 6 m long.
- **Stingrays** get their name from their whip-like tail with its poisonous barbs. A sting from a stingray can make humans very ill.
- **Electric rays** are tropical rays able to give off a powerful electric charge to defend themselves against attackers.
- **The black torpedo ray** can put out a 220 volt shock – as much as a household electric socket.

◄ *The manta ray is also known as the devil ray because the two fleshy flaps on the head were thought to look like horns. The flaps scoop water into the mouth as the manta swims by powerfully beating its vast 'wings'.*

Eels

▼ A gulper eel is about to tackle the head of a
dead fish that has drifted down to the sea floor.
A dragonfish passes by with caution – the gulper
at 60 cm in length is a relative giant of the depths.

- **Eels** are long, slimy fish that look like snakes.

- **Baby eels** are called elvers.

- **Some eels** live in rivers, but most live in the sea, including moray eels and conger eels.

- **Moray eels** are huge and live in tropical waters, hunting fish, squid and cuttlefish.

- **Gulper eels** can live more than 7,500 m down in the Atlantic Ocean. Their mouths are huge to help them catch food in the dark, deep water – so big that they can swallow fish larger than themselves whole.

- **Every autumn,** some European common eels migrate more than 7,000 km, from the Baltic Sea in Europe to the Sargasso Sea near the West Indies to lay their eggs.

- **Migrating eels** are thought to find their way partly by detecting weak electric currents created by the movement of the water.

- **When European eels** hatch in the Sargasso Sea they are carried northeast by the ocean current, developing as they go into tiny transparent eels called glass eels.

- **The electric eels** of South America can produce an electric shock of over 500 volts – enough to knock over an adult human.

- **Garden eels** live in colonies on the seabed, poking out from holes in the sand to catch food drifting by. Their colonies look like gardens of weird plants.

▼ *The common eel can be found in rivers, lakes and even ditches.*

Salmon

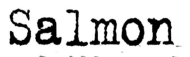

▲ *At sea salmon grow up to as much as 1.5 m long, becoming powerful and fast as they feed on smaller fish.*

● **Salmon** are river and sea fish caught or farmed in huge quantities for food.

● **All salmon** are born in rivers and lakes far inland, then swim down river and out to sea.

● **Adult salmon** spend anything from 6 months to 7 years in the oceans, before returning to rivers and swimming upstream to spawn (lay their eggs).

● **More than five salmon species,** including the sockeye and the chinook, spawn in North American rivers running into the North Pacific.

● **Cherry salmon** spawn in eastern Asian rivers, and amago salmon spawn in Japanese rivers.

- **Atlantic salmon** spawn in rivers in northern Europe and eastern Canada.

- **Spawning salmon** return to the same stream they were born in, up to 3,000 km inland. They are probably sensitive to the chemical and mineral make-up of streams and rivers, helping them to recognise their own stream.

- **To reach their spawning grounds,** salmon have to swim upstream against strong currents, often leaping as high as 5 m to clear waterfalls.

- **When salmon** reach their spawning grounds, they mate. The female lays up to 20,000 eggs.

- **After spawning,** the weakened salmon head down river again, but few make it as far as the sea.

▲ *Salmon returning to their spawning ground make mighty leaps up raging torrents. The journey can take months.*

Ocean fish

- **Nearly 75%** of all fish live in the seas and oceans.

- **The biggest, fastest swimming fish,** such as swordfish and marlin, live near the surface of the open ocean, far from land. They often migrate vast distances to spawn (lay their eggs) or find food.

- **Many smaller fish** live deeper down, including seabed-dwellers like eels and flatfish (such as plaice, turbot and flounders).

▲ *The blue-fin tuna can grow to a massive 4 m in length and 700 kg in weight. It lives in all seas and oceans but moves around with the seasons.*

◄ Flying fish beat their tails so fast they are able to 'fly' away from predators.

- **Flatfish** start life as normal-shaped fish. As they grow older, one eye slowly slides around the head to join the other. The pattern of scales also changes so that one side is the top and one side is the bottom.

- **Plaice** lie on the seabed on their left side, while turbot lie on their right side. Some flounders lie on their left and some on their right.

- **The upper side** of a flatfish is usually camouflaged to help it blend in with the sea floor.

- **In the temperate waters** of the Atlantic there are rich fishing grounds for fish such as herring.

- **The swordfish** can swim at up to 80 km/h. It uses its long spike to stab squid.

- **The bluefin tuna** can grow to as long as 3 m and weigh more than 500 kg. It is also a fast swimmer – one crossed the Atlantic in 199 days.

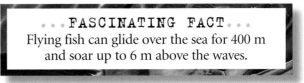

...**FASCINATING FACT**...
Flying fish can glide over the sea for 400 m
and soar up to 6 m above the waves.

Strange deep-sea creatures

- **Deep-sea anglerfish** live deep down in the ocean where it is pitch black. They lure prey into their mouths using a special fishing-rod-like fin spine with a light at its tip.

- **Anglerfish** cannot find each other easily in the dark, so when a male meets a female he stays with her until mating time.

- **Hatchet fish** have giant eyeballs that point upwards so they see prey from below as silhouettes against the surface.

▼ *The viperfish looks fearsome and is one of the larger predators of the ocean depths. Yet it is only 30 cm long. The general lack of food in the deep means animals are mostly small.*

- **Viperfish** shine in the dark, thousands of metres down, and look like a jet airliner at night, with rows of lights along their bodies.

- **Siphonophores** are colonies of tiny creatures that live in the deep oceans. They string themselves together in lines 20 m long and glow – so they look like fairy lights.

- **The cirrate octopod** looks like a jelly because its skin is 95% water – the water cannot be crushed by the intense pressure of the deep oceans where it lives.

▲ *The porcupine fish inflates like a spiny balloon.*

- **The weedy seadragon** of Australia is a seahorse, but it looks just like a piece of flapping seaweed.

- **The sleeper shark** lives in the freezing depths of the North Atlantic and Arctic Oceans. This shark is 6.5 m long, but very slow and sluggish.

- **Flashlight fish** have light organs made by billions of bacteria which shine like headlights. The fish can suddenly block off these lights and change direction in the dark to confuse predators.

- **In the Arab-Israeli War** of 1967 a shoal of flashlight fish was mistaken for enemy frogmen and blown right out of the water.

61

Coral reef fish

- **Many fish species** live in warm seas around coral reefs. They are often very colourful, which makes them instantly recognizable to their own kind.

- **Butterfly fish and angelfish** have slender, oval bodies and are also popular as aquarium fish.

- **Male triggerfish** boost their colour to attract females.

- **Cuckoo wrasse** are all born female, but big females change sex when they are between 7 and 13 years old.

- **Cleaner fish** are the health clinics of the oceans. Larger fish such as groupers queue up for cleaner fish to go over them, nibbling away pests and dead skin.

▲ *The long, sharp fin spines of the lionfish are very poisonous.*

- **The banded coral shrimp** cleans up pests in the same way as cleaner fish do, from fish such as moray eels.

- **The sabre-toothed blenny** looks so like a cleaner fish that it can nip in close to big fish but then it takes a bite out of them.

- **Cheilinus** is a carnivorous fish of coral reefs which changes colour to mimic harmless plant-eating fish, such as parrotfish and goatfish. It swims alongside them, camouflaged, until it is close to its prey.

▼*The gaudy underworld of a healthy coral reef.*

···**FASCINATING FACT**···
Cleaner fish will go to work inside
a shark's mouth.

63

Seals and sea lions

- **Seals, sea lions and walruses** are sea mammals that mainly live in water and are agile swimmers, but which waddle awkwardly when they come on land.

- **Most seals** eat fish, squid and shellfish. Crabeater seals eat mainly shrimps, not crabs.

- **Seals and sea lions** have ears, but only sea lions (and fur seals) have ear flaps.

- **Only sea lions** can move their back flippers under their body when travelling about on land.

- **When seals come ashore** to breed, they live for weeks in vast colonies called rookeries.

◄ The harp seal is so-called because the black marks on the seal's back are supposed to resemble the shape of the musical instrument.

- **Walruses** are bigger and bulkier than seals, and they have massive tusks and face whiskers.

- **When hunters kill seal pups** for their fur, or to keep numbers down, it is called culling.

- **Elephant seals** spend up to 8 months far out in the ocean continuously diving, with each dive lasting 20 minutes or so.

- **There are freshwater seals** in Lake Baikal in Russia.

▼ *Seal pups (babies) like this one grow a thick, furry coat.*

.....FASCINATING FACT... .
The 4 m-long leopard seal of Antarctica
feeds on penguins and even other seals.

Whales

- **Whales,** dolphins and porpoises are large mammals called cetaceans that live mostly in the seas and oceans. Dolphins and porpoises are small whales.

- **Like all mammals**, whales have lungs – this means they have to come to the surface to breathe every 10 minutes or so, although they can stay down for up to 40 minutes. A sperm whale can hold its breath for 2 hours.

- **Whales breathe** through blowholes on top of their head. When a whale breathes out, it spouts out water vapour and mucus. When it breathes in, it sucks in about 2,000 litres of air within about 2 seconds.

- **Like land mammals,** whales nurse their babies with their own milk. Whale milk is so rich that babies grow incredibly fast. Blue whale babies are over 7 m long when they are born and gain an extra 100 kg or so a day for about 7 months.

▶ *Killer whales or orcas are big deep-sea predators, growing to as long as 9 m and weighing up to 10 tonnes. They feed on fish, seals, penguins and dolphins.*

To swim, whales flap their fluke (tail) up and down

Dorsal fin

▶ *Humpback whales live together in groups called pods and keep in touch with their own 'dialect' of noises.*

- **Toothed whales,** such as the sperm whale and the orca or killer whale, have teeth and prey on large fish and seals. The six groups of toothed whale are sperm whales, beaked whales, belugas and narwhals, dolphins, porpoises, and river dolphins.

- **Baleen whales,** such as the humpback and blue, have a comb of thin plates called baleen in place of teeth. They feed by straining small, shrimp-like creatures called krill through their baleen. There are five baleen whale groups, including right whales, grey whales and rorquals. Rorquals have grooves on their throats and include humpback, minke and blue whales.

- **The blue whale** is the largest creature that ever lived. Blue whales grow to be over 30 m long and weigh more than 150 tonnes. In summer, they eat over 4 tonnes of krill every day – that is 4 million krill.

- **Whales keep in touch** with sounds called phonations. Large baleen whales make sounds which are too low for humans to hear, but they can be heard by other whales at least 80 km away.

- **Most baleen whales** live alone or in small groups, but toothed whales – especially dolphins – often swim together in groups called pods or schools.

> ...**FASCINATING FACT**...
> Male humpbacks make elaborate 'songs' lasting
> 20 minutes or more – perhaps to woo females.

Dolphins

▶ *Fraser's dolphin is of average size at 2.3 m long and 85 kg in weight. Like all dolphins it makes clicks to find its way by echolocation.*

- **Dolphins** are sea creatures that belong to the same family as whales – the cetaceans.

- **Dolphins are mammals,** not fish. They are warm-blooded, and mothers feed their young on milk.

- **There are two kinds** of dolphin – marine (sea) dolphins (32 species) and river dolphins (5 species).

- **Dolphins usually live** in groups of 20 to 100 animals.

- **Dolphins look after** each other. Often, they will support an injured companion on the surface.

- **Dolphins communicate** with high-pitched clicks called phonations. Some clicks are higher than any other animal noise and humans cannot hear them.

- **Dolphins use sound** to find things and can identify different objects even when blindfolded.

- **Dolphins can be trained** to jump through hoops, toss balls, or 'walk' backwards through the water on their tails.

- **Bottle-nosed dolphins** get their name from their short beaks (which also make them look like they are smiling). They are friendly and often swim near boats.

▼ *Dolphins have rescued drowning humans by pushing them to the surface.*

Reptiles and amphibians

- **Reptiles** are scaly-skinned animals which live in many different habitats mainly in warm regions . They include crocodiles, lizards, snakes and tortoises.

- **Reptiles are cold-blooded,** but this does not mean that their blood is cold. A reptile's body cannot keep its blood warm, and it has to control its temperature by moving between hot and cool places.

◄ *Like all reptiles, crocodiles rely on basking in the sun to gain energy for hunting. At night, or when it is cold, they usually sleep.*

Newts are amphibians. The long, fin-like crest on the back of this great crested newt becomes taller and more colourful in spring when the male attracts a female for mating. This large newt measures 17 cm.

● **Reptiles bask in the sun** to gain energy to hunt, and are often less active at cooler times of year.

● **A reptile's skin** looks slimy, but it is quite dry. It keeps in moisture so well that reptiles can survive in deserts. The skin often turns darker to absorb the sun's heat.

● **Although reptiles grow** for most of their lives, their skin does not, so they must slough (shed) it every now and then.

● **Amphibians** are animals that live both on land and in water. They include frogs, toads, newts and salamanders.

● **Most reptiles** lay their eggs on land, but amphibians hatch out in water as tadpoles, from huge clutches of eggs called spawn.

● **Like fish,** tadpoles have gills to breathe in water, but they soon metamorphose (change), growing legs and lungs.

● **Amphibians** never stray far from water.

> ····FASCINATING FACT····
> Reptiles were the first large creatures to live entirely on land, over 350 million years ago.

Dinosaurs

- **Dinosaurs** were reptiles that dominated life on land from about 220 million to 65 million years ago, when all of them mysteriously became extinct.

- **Although modern reptiles** walk with bent legs splayed out, dinosaurs had straight legs under their bodies – this meant they could run fast or grow heavy.

- **Some dinosaurs** ran on their back two legs, as birds do. Others had four sturdy legs like an elephant's.

- **Dinosaurs** are split into two groups according to their hipbones – saurischians had reptile-like hips and ornithischians had bird-like hips.

▶ Stegosaurus *had a tiny skull relative to its body size, and a brain the size of a walnut. It had rows of plates along its back with four long spines at the end of its tail.*

◄ *Dinosaur means 'terrible lizard', and they came in all shapes and sizes. This is a plant-eating sauropod called* Diplodocus.

- **Saurischians** were either swift, two-legged predators called theropods, or hefty four-legged herbivores called sauropods.

- **Theropods** had acute eyesight, fearsome claws and sharp teeth. They included *Tyrannosaurus rex*, one of the biggest hunting animals to ever live on land – over 15 m long, 5 m tall and weighing more than 7 tonnes.

- **Sauropods** had massive bodies, long tails, and long, snake-like necks.

- **The sauropod *Brachiosaurus*** was over 23 m long, weighed 80 tonnes and towered 12 m into the air. It was one of the biggest creature ever to live on land.

- **Most dinosaurs** are known from fossilized bones, but fossilized eggs, footprints and droppings have also been found. In 1913, mummified hadrosaur skin was found.

- **Some scientists** think the dinosaurs died out after a huge meteor struck Earth off Mexico, creating a cloud that blocked the sun's light and heat.

Turtles and tortoises

- **Turtles and tortoises** are reptiles that live inside hard, armoured shells. Together with terrapins, they make up a group called the chelonians.

- **Turtles** live in the sea, freshwater, or on land, tortoises live on land, and terrapins live in streams and lakes.

- **The shield** on the back of a chelonian is called a carapace. Its flat belly armour is called a plastron.

- **Most turtles and tortoises** eat plants and tiny animals. They have no teeth, just jaws with very sharp edges.

▲ *Tortoises are very slow moving and placid.*

- **Tortoises** live mostly in hot, dry regions and will hibernate in winter if brought to a cold country.

- **Turtles and tortoises** live to a great age. One giant tortoise found in 1766 in Mauritius lived 152 years.

- **The giant tortoise** grows to as long as 1.5 m.

- **The leatherback turtle** grows to as long as 2.5 m and weighs more than 800 kg.

- **Every three years,** green turtles gather together to swim thousands of kilometres to Ascension Island in the mid-Atlantic, where they lay their eggs ashore by moonlight at the highest tide. They bury the eggs in the sand, to be incubated by the heat of the sun.

▼ *The spotted turtle largely lives and feeds in water. It will eat fish, water snails and other animals.*

carapace

.....FASCINATING FACT.....
Giant tortoises were once kept on ships
to provide fresh meat on long voyages.

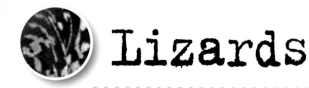

Lizards

- **Lizards** are a group of 3,800 scaly-skinned reptiles, varying from a few centimetres long to the 3 m-long Komodo dragon.

- **Lizards cannot** control their own body heat, and so rely on sunshine for warmth. This is why they live in warm climates and bask in the sun for hours each day.

- **Lizards move** in many ways – running, scampering and slithering. Some can glide. Unlike mammals, their limbs stick out sideways rather than downwards.

- **Most lizards** lay eggs, although a few give birth to live young. But unlike birds or mammals, a mother lizard does not nurture (look after) her young.

- **Most lizards** are meat-eaters, feeding on insects and other small creatures.

▲ *Lizards have four legs and a long tail. In most lizards, the back legs are much stronger than the front, and are used to drive the animal forwards in a kind of writhing motion.*

▶ *Geckos are small lizards that are mainly active at night. Their toes are are covered in hairy pads, which help them to stick to rough surfaces. Some geckos can even walk upside down.*

- **The glass lizard** has no legs. Its tail may break off and lie wriggling as a decoy if it is attacked. The lizard later grows another one.

- **The Australian frilled lizard** has a ruff around its neck. To put off attackers, it can spread out its ruff to make itself look three or four times bigger.

- **Horned lizards** can squirt a jet of blood from their eyes almost as far as 1 m to put off attackers.

- **The Komodo dragon** of Sumatra is the biggest lizard, weighing up to 150 kg or more. It can catch deer and pigs and swallow them whole.

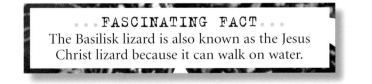

. . . FASCINATING FACT . . .
The Basilisk lizard is also known as the Jesus Christ lizard because it can walk on water.

77

Iguanas

- **Iguanas** are large lizards that live around the Pacific and in the Americas.

- **Larger iguanas** are the only vegetarian lizards. Unlike other lizards, most eat fruit, flowers and leaves, rather than insects.

- **The common iguana** lives high up in trees, but lays its eggs in a hole in the ground.

▼ *Before each dive into water, marine iguanas warm themselves in the sun to gain energy.*

- **Common iguanas** will jump 6 m or more out of the trees to the ground if they are disturbed.

- **The rhinoceros iguana** of the West Indies gets its name from the pointed scales on its snout.

- **The marine iguana** of the Galapagos Islands is the only lizard that spends much of its life in the sea.

- **Marine iguanas** keep their eggs warm ready for hatching in the mouth of volcanoes, risking death to put them there.

- **When in the water,** a marine iguana may dive for 15 minutes or more, pushing itself along with its tail.

- **Although marine iguanas** cannot breathe underwater, their heart rate slows so that they use less oxygen.

- **The chuckwalla** inflates its body with air to wedge itself in a rock crack if it is in danger.

▶ *There are 700 plus species of iguana, nearly all of which live in the Americas. Like most lizards, iguanas hatch from eggs.*

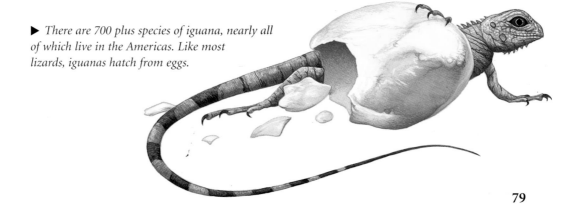

Chameleons

- **Chameleons** are 85 species of lizard, most of which live on the island of Madagascar and in mainland Africa.

- **The smallest chameleon**, the dwarf Brookesia, could balance on your little finger. The biggest, Oustalet's chameleon, is the size of a small cat.

- **A chameleon** can look forwards and backwards at the same time, as each of its amazing eyes can swivel in all directions independently of the other.

- **Chameleons feed** on insects and spiders, hunting them in trees by day.

- **A chameleon's tongue** is almost as long as its body, but is normally squashed up inside its mouth.

▼ *The chameleon can shoot out its tongue to a great length.*

▶ *Most of a chameleon's bulging eyes are protected by skin.*

- **A chameleon shoots** out its tongue in a fraction of a second to trap its victim on a sticky pad at the tip.

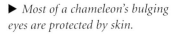

- **The chameleon's tongue** is fired out from a special launching bone on its lower jaw.

- **Most lizards** can change colour, but chameleons are experts, changing quickly to all sorts of colours.

- **Chameleons change colour** when they are angry or frightened, too cold or too hot, or sick – but they change colour less often to match their surroundings.

- **The colour** of the skin is controlled by pigment cells called melanophores, which change colour as they change size.

81

Pythons and boas

- **Constrictors** are snakes that squeeze their victims to death, rather than poisoning them. They include pythons, boas and anacondas.

- **A constrictor** does not crush its victim. Instead, it winds itself around, gradually tightening its coils until the victim suffocates.

- **Constrictors usually swallow** victims whole, then spend days digesting them. They have special jaws that allow their mouths to open very wide. A large meal can be seen as a lump moving down the body.

▼ *Pythons are tropical snakes that live in moist forests in Asia and Africa. They are the world's biggest snakes, rivalled only by giant anacondas. Pythons are one long tube of muscle, well able to squeeze even big victims to death. They usually eat animals about the size of domestic cats, but occasionally they go for really big meals such as wild pigs and deer.*

- **Pythons** are big snakes that live in Asia, Indonesia and Africa. In captivity, reticulated pythons grow to 9 m. Boas and anacondas are the big constrictors of South America.

- **Boas** capture their prey by lying in wait, hiding motionless under trees and waiting for victims to pass by. But like all snakes, they can go for many weeks without eating.

- **Like many snakes**, most constrictors begin life as eggs. Unusually for snakes, female pythons look after their eggs until they hatch by coiling around them. Even more unusually, Indian and green tree pythons actually keep their eggs warm by shivering.

- **Female boas** do not lay eggs, giving birth to live young.

- **Boas** have tiny remnants of back legs, called spurs, which males use to tickle females during mating.

- **Anacondas** spend much of their lives in swampy ground or shallow water, lying in wait for victims to come and drink. One anaconda was seen to swallow a 2 m-long caiman (a kind of crocodile).

- **When frightened,** the royal python of Africa coils itself into a tight ball, which is why it is sometimes called the ball python. Rubber boas do the same, but hide their heads and stick their tails out aggressively to fool attackers.

> **. . . FASCINATING FACT . . .**
> A 4 to 5 m-long African rock python was
> once seen to swallow an entire 60 kg impala
> (a kind of antelope) whole – horns and all.

Cobras and vipers

● **Two kinds of poisonous snake** are dangerous to humans – vipers and elapids such as cobras and mambas.

● **Elapids** have their venom (poison) in short front fangs. A viper's fangs are so long that they usually have to be folded away.

● **The hamadryad cobra** of Southeast Asia is the world's largest poisonous snake, growing to over 5 m.

● **In India, cobras kill** more than 7,000 people every year. The bite of a king cobra can kill an elephant in 4 hours. The marine cobra lives in the sea and its venom is 100 times more deadly.

● **Snake charmers** use the spectacled cobra, playing to it so that it follows the pipe as if about to strike – but the snake's fangs have been removed to make it safe.

▶ *When on the defensive, a cobra rears up and spreads the skin of its neck in a hood to make it look bigger. This often gives victims a chance to hit it away.*

● **A spitting cobra** squirts venom into its attacker's eyes, and is accurate at 2 m or more. The venom is not deadly, but it blinds the victim and is very painful.

- **The black mamba** of Africa can race along at 25 km/h with its head raised and its tongue flickering.

- **A viper's venom** kills its victims by making their blood clot. Viper venom has been used to treat haemophiliacs (people whose blood does not clot well).

- **The pit vipers** of the Americas hunt their warm-blooded victims using heat-sensitive pits on the side of their heads (see animal senses).

▶ *The wedge-shaped head, narrow neck and brown-green scale pattern of the Gaboon viper make this snake almost impossible to spot among the leaves of the forest floor. It has the longest fangs of any viper, up to 5 cm.*

. . . **FASCINATING FACT** . . .
Fer-de-lance snakes have 60 to 80 babies, each of which is deadly poisonous.

85

Crocodiles and alligators

- **Crocodiles, alligators, caimans and gharials** are large reptiles that together form the group known as crocodilians. There are 14 species of crocodile, 7 alligators and caimans, and 1 gharial.

- **Crocodilian species** lived alongside the dinosaurs 200 million years ago, and they are the nearest we have to living dinosaurs today.

- **Crocodilians are hunters** that lie in wait for animals coming to drink at the water's edge. When crocodilians seize a victim they drag it into the water, stun it with a blow from their tail, then drown it.

- **Like all reptiles,** crocodilians get their energy from the sun. Typically, they bask in the sun on a sandbar or the river bank in the morning, then slip into the river at midday to cool off.

▶ *Crocodiles are huge reptiles with powerful bodies, scaly skin and great snapping jaws.*

The crocodile's eyes and nostrils are raised so it can see and breathe while floating under water

A crocodile will often kill its victims with a swipe from its strong tail

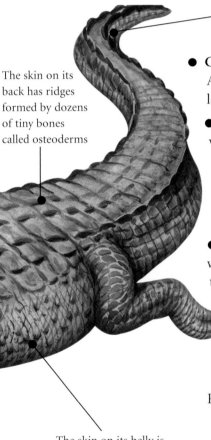

The skin on its back has ridges formed by dozens of tiny bones called osteoderms

The skin on its belly is smooth and was once prized as a material for shoes and handbags

● **Crocodiles live** in tropical rivers and swamps. At over 5 m long, saltwater crocodiles are the world's largest reptiles – one grew to over 8 m long.

● **Crocodiles** are often said to cry after eating their victims. In fact only saltwater crocodiles cry, and they do it to get rid of salt, not because they are sorry.

● **Crocodiles have thinner snouts** than alligators, and a fourth tooth on the lower jaw which is visible when the crocodile's mouth is shut.

● **The female Nile crocodile** lays her eggs in nests which she digs in sandy river banks, afterwards covering the eggs in sand to keep them at a steady temperature. When the babies hatch they make loud piping calls. The mother then digs them out and carries them one by one in her mouth to the river.

● **Alligators** are found both in the Florida Everglades in the United States and in the Yangtze River in China.

...**FASCINATING FACT**...
Crocodilians often swallow stones to help them stay underwater for long periods. Without this ballast, they might tip over.

87

Frogs and toads

- **Frogs** and toads are amphibians – creatures that live both on land and in the water.

- **There are about 3,500 species** of frog and toad. Most live near water, but some live in trees and others live underground.

- **Frogs** are mostly smaller and better jumpers. Toads are bigger, with thicker, wartier skin which holds on to moisture and allows them to live on land longer.

◄ Frogs are superb jumpers, with long back legs to propel them into the air. Most also have suckers on their fingers to help them land securely on slippery surfaces.

- **Frogs and toads** are meat-eaters. They catch fast-moving insects by darting out their long, sticky tongues.

- **Frogs and toads begin life** as fish-like tadpoles, hatching in the water from huge clutches of eggs called spawn.

- **After 7 to 10 weeks**, tadpoles grow legs and lungs and develop into frogs ready to leave the water.

- **In midwife toads,** the male looks after the eggs, not the female – winding strings of eggs around his back legs and carrying them about until they hatch.

- **The male Darwin's frog** swallows the eggs and keeps them in his throat until they hatch – and pop out of his mouth.

- **The goliath frog** of West Africa is the largest frog – at over 25 cm long. The biggest toad is the cane toad of Queensland, Australia – one weighed 2.6 kg and measured 50 cm in length with its legs outstretched. The cane toad was introduced to Australia from South America to help control pests.

- **The arrow-poison frogs** that live in the tropical rainforests of Central America get their name because natives tip their arrows with deadly poison from glands in the frogs' skin. Many arrow-poison frogs are very colourful.

▶ *The natterjack toad is easily recognized by a distinctive yellow line down its head and back. It gives off a smell of burning rubber when alarmed.*

89

What are birds?

◄ One of Europe's smallest birds, the wren is found in many habitats from open moor to dense marsh. It holds its tail almost upright and builds a domed nest among tree roots.

- **Not all birds** can fly, but they all have feathers.
- **Feathers** are light, but they are linked by hooks called barbs to make them strong enough for flight.
- **Wrens** have 1,000 feathers, while swans have 20,000.
- **Birds have four kinds** of wing feather – large primaries, smaller secondaries, coverts and contours.
- **Every kind of bird** has its own formation pattern and colour of feathers, called its plumage.
- **Instead of a teeth,** birds have a hard beak or bill.
- **Unlike humans,** birds do not give birth to babies. Instead they lay eggs, usually sitting on them to keep them warm until they hatch (see birds' nests and eggs).
- **Birds fly in two ways** – by gliding with their wings held still, or by flapping their wings up and down.
- **Gliding is less effort** than flapping, and birds that stay in the air a long time tend to be superb gliders – including birds of prey, swifts, gulls and gannets.
- **Albatrosses and petrels** have long narrow wings that help them sail upwards on rising air currents.

▼ *Most birds flap their wings to fly. Even birds that spend much of their time gliding have to flap their wings to take off and land.*

····FASCINATING FACT····
Birds may be descended from dinosaurs and
took to the air 150 million years ago.

91

Ostriches and emus

- **Ratites are big, flightless birds** like the ostrich, emu, cassowary, rhea and kiwi. Ratites always walk or run everywhere, only using their small wings for balance and for show.

- **The ostrich** is the biggest living bird, towering up to 2.75 m in height and weighing over 150 kg.

- **To escape a lion,** the ostrich can hurtle over the African savannah grasslands, where it lives, at speeds of 60 km/h – faster than a racehorse. Even when the ostrich tires, its strong legs can still deliver a massive kick.

▼ *Ostriches live on the grasslands of Africa and nest in holes scooped out of the ground. The male scoops out the hole and leads several females to it to lay their eggs.*

- **Ostriches** have only two toes on each foot – unlike the rhea of South America which has three.

- **The ostrich lays** the largest egg – almost as big as a football.

Two toes with very sharp toenails

◀ *The emu of Australia is the world's second largest bird, growing up to 1.7 m tall and weighing upto 45 kg.*

- **The kiwi of New Zealand** is the smallest ratite, no bigger than a chicken. It has fur-like feathers and is the only bird with nostrils at the tip of its bill, which it uses to sniff out worms and grubs.

- **The rare kakapo parrot** of New Zealand could fly once, but it lost the power of flight because it had no natural predators – until Europeans introduced dogs and cats to New Zealand.

- **The dodo** was a flightless bird that once lived on islands such as Mauritius in the Indian Ocean. It was wiped out in the 17th century when its eggs were eaten by pigs and monkeys imported by Europeans.

- **The emu** of Australia is the best swimmer of any flightless bird. Ostriches can swim well, too.

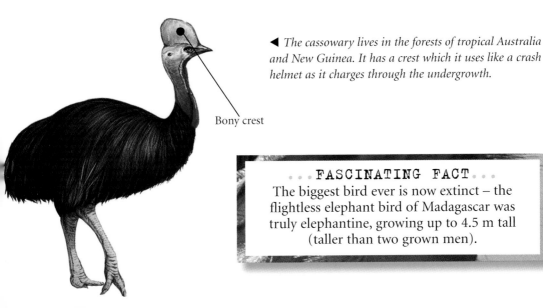

◀ *The cassowary lives in the forests of tropical Australia and New Guinea. It has a crest which it uses like a crash helmet as it charges through the undergrowth.*

Bony crest

. . . FASCINATING FACT . . .
The biggest bird ever is now extinct – the
flightless elephant bird of Madagascar was
truly elephantine, growing up to 4.5 m tall
(taller than two grown men).

Pheasants and peafowl

- **A game bird** is a bird that is hunted for sport.

- **Game birds** spend most of the time strutting along the ground looking for seeds. They fly only in emergencies.

- **There are 250 species** of game bird, including pheasants, grouse, partridges, quails, wild turkeys and peafowl.

- **Most of the 48 species** of pheasant originated in China and central Asia.

▶ *The peacock (the male peafowl) of India and Sri Lanka is the most spectacular of all pheasants. When courting the drab peahen, the peacock throws up his tail feathers to create a gigantic turquoise fan.*

▶ *The common partridge is familiar as a game bird on farm land in Europe and south-western Asia. Partridges eat seeds and young shoots which they find on the ground.*

● **Many hen (female) game birds** have dull brown plumage that helps them to hide in their woodland and moorland homes.

● **Many cock (male) game birds** have very colourful plumage to attract mates.

● **In the breeding season,** cocks strut and puff up their plumage to attract a mate. They also draw attention to themselves by cackling, whistling and screaming.

● **Pheasant cocks** often fight each other violently to win a particular mating area.

● **The jungle fowl** of Southeast Asia is the wild ancestor of the domestic chicken.

● **Peacocks** were carried as treasure from India throughout the ancient world.

95

Turkeys and hens

- **Turkeys,** chickens, geese and ducks are all kinds of poultry – farm birds bred to provide meat, eggs and feathers.

- **Chickens** were first tamed 5,000 years ago, and there are now over 200 breeds, including bantams and Rhode Island reds.

- **Female chickens** and turkeys are called hens. Male chickens are called roosters or cockerels. Male turkeys are toms. Baby turkeys are poults.

◀ *The wild turkey of North America lives in forest and scrub, where it feeds on the ground eating seeds, nuts and berries. At night it flaps in branches to rest.*

▶ *Roosters are renowned for their noisy cries every morning as the sun comes up. This harsh cry is called a crow.*

- **To keep hens laying,** their eggs must be collected daily. If not, the hens will wait until they have a small clutch of eggs, then try to sit on them to hatch them.

- **Battery hens** spend their lives crowded into rows of cages called batteries inside buildings.

- **Free-range hens** are allowed to scratch outdoors for insects and seeds.

- **Chickens** raised only for eating are called broilers.

- **Turkeys** are a kind of pheasant. There are several species, but all are descended from the native wild turkey of North America, first tamed by Native Americans 1,000 years ago.

- **Male turkeys** have a loose fold of bare, floppy skin called a wattle hanging down from their head and neck.

...**FASCINATING FACT**...
All domestic chickens are descended from
the wild red jungle fowl of India.

Ducks and geese

- **Ducks, geese and swans** are known as waterfowl, and they all live on or near freshwater.

- **Waterfowl** can float for hours and have webbed feet for paddling along. On water they are graceful, but on land they waddle awkwardly, since their legs are set far back under their body for swimming.

- **Ducks** have shorter necks and wings, and flatter bills than swans. Male ducks are called drakes, and females, ducks. Babies are called ducklings.

▼ *The ruddy duck has a stiff tail held up at an angle. The male's courtship display involves rapid paddling as he holds his head against his chest.*

▶ *Canada geese breed in the far north of Canada and Alaska, and migrate south to warmer regions in the autumn.*

- **Diving ducks** (such as the pochard, tufted duck and the scoter) dive for food such as roots, shellfish and insects on the river bed.

- **Dabbling ducks** (such as the mallard, widgeon, gadwall and the teal) dabble – they sift water through their beaks for food.

- **Some dabblers** lap water at the surface. Others up-end – sticking their heads into the water to sift out water weeds and snails from muddy water.

- **Swans** are the largest waterfowl. They have long elegant necks and pure white plumage – apart from the black-neck swan of South America and the Australian black swan.

- **Baby swans** are called cygnets and are mottled grey.

- **Geese** mostly graze on grass. Unlike ducks, which quack and swans which hiss, geese honk.

- **Baby geese** are called goslings.

99

Woodpeckers and toucans

▶ *The black-headed woodpecker is a noisy bird with a loud, squawking call in flight, when its bright red rump contrasts with the green body and red-capped black head.*

- **Woodpeckers** are closely related to the colourful toucans and jacamars of tropical rainforests.

- **Woodpeckers,** toucans, barbets, jacamars and honeyguides all have two toes on each foot pointing forwards and two pointing backwards. Their toes help them cling to trees and branches.

- **Woodpeckers** use their powerful bills to bore into tree trunks to get at insects. They spear the insects with their incredibly long tongues.

- **Gila woodpeckers** escape the desert heat by nesting inside giant saguaro cacti (where it can be 30°C cooler).

- **Redhead woodpeckers** drill holes in trees and use them to store acorns for winter – wedging them in very tightly so that squirrels cannot steal them.

- **Woodpeckers** claim their territory not by singing, but by hammering their bills against trees.

- **Honeyguides** lead honey badgers to bees' nests. The badger opens them to get the honey and the bird gets beeswax.

- **When toucans sleep**, they turn their heads around and lay their bills down their backs.

▲ *The toucan's giant beak is full of air holes, so it is not heavy enough to overbalance the bird. Toucans eat mainly small fruit.*

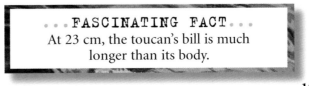

...FASCINATING FACT...
At 23 cm, the toucan's bill is much longer than its body.

101

Parrots and budgerigars

▲ *The blue-and-yellow macaw of the Amazon rainforest has been trapped so much for the pet trade, it is now quite rare.*

- **Parrots** are colourful birds with curved bills for eating fruits and seeds and for cracking nuts. They are very noisy birds and they live mostly in tropical rainforests.

- **Parrots** have feet with two toes pointing forwards and two backwards, allowing them to grip branches and hold food.

- **There are 330 or so parrot species** divided into three main groups – true parrots, cockatoos and lories.

- **Half of all parrot species,** including macaws, green Amazon parrots and parakeets, live in Latin America.

- **Australia and New Guinea** are home to parrots called cockatoos (which are white with feathered crests on their heads), as well as to lories and lorikeets.

- **The budgerigar** is a small parakeet from central Australia which is very popular as a pet.

The pink cockatoo's headcrest displays bands of scarlet and yellow when spread

- **The hanging parrots** of Southeast Asia get their name because they sleep upside down like bats.

- **The kea** of New Zealand is a parrot that eats meat as well as fruit. It was once wrongly thought to be a sheep killer.

- **Parrots** are well known for their mimicry of human voices. Some have a repertoire of 300 words or more.

- **An African grey parrot** called Alex was trained by scientist Irene Pepperberg to identify at least 50 different objects. Alex could ask for each of these objects in English – and also refuse them.

▶ *The white plumage of the pink cockatoo is shot through with a soft pink flush.*

Swifts and hummingbirds

- **Swifts and hummingbirds** are on the wing so much that their feet have become weak – which is why they are called Apodiformes, meaning 'footless ones'.

- **Swifts** are among the fastest flying birds. Spine-tailed swifts of eastern Asia have been recorded at 240 km/h.

- **Swifts use** their short, gaping bills to catch insects on the wing.

- **Swifts may fly** through the night without landing. They may even sleep on the wing. European swifts fly all the way to Africa and back without stopping.

- **When swifts land,** they cling to vertical surfaces such as walls, cliffs and trees.

- **Great dusky swifts** nest and roost behind waterfalls, and have to fly through the water to get in and out.

- **Hummingbirds** are 325 species of tiny, colourful, tropical birds which sip nectar from flowers.

- **Hummingbirds** are the most amazing aerial acrobats, hovering and twisting in front of flowers.

- **The bee hummingbird** is the world's smallest bird – including its long bill, it measures just 5 cm.

▲ *Swifts winter in Africa, then fly north and east to Europe and Asia to breed. Their feet are so small and weak that they can hardly perch on twigs.*

▼ *Hummingbirds have long bills to suck nectar from flowers.*

. . . **FASCINATING FACT** . . .
To hover, horned sungem
hummingbirds beat their
wings 90 times per second.

105

Owls

- **Owls** are nocturnal and hunt by night, unlike most other hunting birds.

- **There are two big families of owl** – barn owls and typical owls.

- **There are 135 species** of typical owl, including the great horned owl.

- **There are about 10 species** of barn owl. The common barn owl is the most widespread – found on every continent except Antarctica.

- **Small owls** eat mostly insects. Bigger owls eat mice and shrews. Eagle owls can catch young deer.

- **In the country,** the tawny owl's diet is 90% small mammals, but many now live in towns where their diet is mainly small birds such as sparrows and starlings.

▲ *An owl's big eyes face straight forward to focus on an object. However, owls cannot move their eyes and have to swivel their whole head to look to the side or rear.*

◄ *Most owls roost by day in holes inside tree trunks. There are few trees in the desert where the elf owl lives, so it roosts inside a giant saguaro cactus. Elf owls live in the dry regions of southwest North America.*

- **Owls have huge eyes** that allow them to see in almost pitch darkness.

- **An owl's hearing** is four times as sharp as a cat's.

- **Owls can pinpoint** sounds with astonishing accuracy from the slight difference in the sound levels it receives in each of its ears.

- **Most bird's eyes** look out to the sides, but an owl's look straight forward like a human's. This is probably why the owl has been a symbol of wisdom since ancient times.

- **The flight feathers** on an owl's wing muffle the sound of the bird's wingbeat so that it can swoop almost silently down on to its prey.

107

Seagulls and albatrosses

▲ *Seagulls catch small fish, steal eggs and young from other birds, scavenge on waste – and sometimes fly inland to find worms.*

▼ *The wandering albatross can glide for hours without a single flap of its huge wings. It glides quite low, usually less than 20 m above the waves, where rising winds keep it aloft.*

- **Gulls are big sea birds** that live on coasts all around the world, nesting on cliffs, islands or beaches.

- **Gulls are related** to skuas and terns.

- **Skuas** have hooked claws and sharp bills, which they use to attack other birds and force them to disgorge (throw up) their food – which the skua then eats.

- **Skuas are such good acrobats** that they can catch the disgorged meal of another bird in mid-air.

- **The great skua** often pounces on seagulls, drowns them, and then steals their chicks.

- **Wandering albatrosses** are the biggest of all sea birds, with white bodies and dark wings.

- **The wandering albatross** has the biggest wingspan of any bird – 3.7 m across.

- **An albatross** will often follow a ship for days without stopping to rest.

- **Wild albatrosses** may live for more than 50 years.

> ...FASCINATING FACT...
> Herring gulls watch ducks diving for fish
> and then steal it when the ducks resurface.

Eagles and hawks

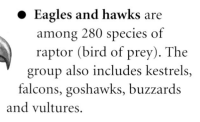

● **Eagles and hawks** are among 280 species of raptor (bird of prey). The group also includes kestrels, falcons, goshawks, buzzards and vultures.

● **Most birds of prey are hunters** that feed on other birds, fish and small mammals.

● **Most birds of prey** are strong fliers, with sharp eyes, powerful talons (claws) and a hooked beak.

● **Birds of prey lay** only one or two eggs at a time. This makes them vulnerable to human egg collectors – one reason why many are endangered species.

● **Eagles** are the biggest of the hunting birds, with wing spans of up to 2.5 m. The harpy eagle of the Amazon catches monkeys and sloths.

▲ *Stellar's sea eagle is one of the most powerful of all birds. It has a wingspan of 2.4 m and a massive beak.*

▲ *The bald eagle eats fish, snatching them from rivers.*

- **The American bald eagle** is not really bald, but has white feathers on its head.

- **There are two kinds of hawks.** Accipiters, like the goshawk, catch their prey by lying in wait on perches. Buteos, like the kestrel, hover in the air.

- **Buzzards** are buteo hawks.

- **In the Middle Ages**, merlins and falcons were trained to fly from a falconer's wrist to catch birds and animals.

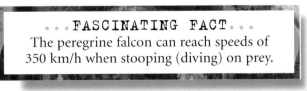

... FASCINATING FACT ...
The peregrine falcon can reach speeds of
350 km/h when stooping (diving) on prey.

111

Vultures

- **Vultures and condors** are the biggest birds of prey. They do not hunt, but feed on carrion (dead animals).

- **The palmnut vulture** is the only vegetarian bird of prey, and it feeds on oil nuts.

- **Many vultures are bald,** with no head feathers to mat with blood when digging into corpses.

- **The seven species** of New World vulture (those that live in the Americas) have a nostril hole right through their beak.

▼ *A vulture closes in to feed on a dead animal.*

112

- **The Californian condor** is very rare. All the wild ones were captured in the mid 1980s, but some have since been bred in captivity and returned to the wild.

- **Vultures** are great fliers and spend hours soaring, scanning the ground for corpses with sharp eyes.

- **Condors** have such a sharp sense of smell that they can pinpoint a corpse under a thick forest canopy.

- **Vultures** have such weak bills that flesh must be rotten before they can eat it.

- **The lammergeier** is known as the bearded vulture because it has a beard of black bristles on its chin.

▼ *The Andean condor holds the bird world record for wing area. It can spot a dead sheep from 5 km away.*

... FASCINATING FACT ...
The Andean condor is the world's biggest flying bird, with a wingspan of 3 m or more.

113

Wading birds

Flamingos' feathers can vary from pale pink to red. Wing feathers are normally black.

- **Herons** are large wading birds that hunt for fish in shallow lakes and rivers. There are about 60 species.

- **When hunting**, a heron stands alone in the water, often on one leg, apparently asleep. Then it makes a lightning dart with its long beak to spear a fish or frog.

▲ *Flamingos live on the shellfish and organisms to be found in the muddy waters of the lakes, marshes and seas where they live. They gather in huge colonies sometimes containing thousands of birds.*

- **Herons** usually nest in colonies called heronries. They build loose stick-nests in trees.

- **Storks** are very large black-and-white water birds with long necks and legs. There are 17 species of stork.

- **The white stork** lives in Eurasia in the summer, and then migrates to Africa, India and southern China in the winter.

114

- **White storks** build twig-nests on roofs, and some people think they bring luck to the house they nest on.

- **Flamingoes** are large pink wading birds which live in huge colonies on tropical lakes.

- **Spoonbills and ibises** are wading birds whose bills are sensitive enough to let them feel their prey moving in the water.

- **There are 28 species** of spoonbill and ibis.

- **The spoonbill's name** comes from its spoon-shaped bill, which it swings through the water to scoop up fish.

▶ *Egrets are large wading birds that live in marshy areas, feeding on fish and insects.*

115

Penguins

- **There are around 17 different species** of penguin, most of them living in colonies called rookeries along the coast of Antarctica and nearby islands.

- **Penguins** are superb swimmers, using their wings as flippers to push them through the water, and steering with their webbed feet.

- **Penguins have coats** waterproofed with oil and thick fat so they can survive in temperatures as low as -60°C.

- **The smallest** is the fairy penguin, at 40 cm high.

▲ Penguins are sociable birds that live in large colonies.

116

- **The emperor penguin** is the biggest swimming bird, at up to 1.2 m tall and weighing over 40 kg – twice the weight of any flying bird.

- **Emperor penguins** can dive briefly to depths of 250 m or more chasing fish, their main diet.

- **Penguins** can leap high out of the water to land on an ice bank, but on land they can only waddle clumsily or toboggan along on their bellies.

- **Adélie penguins** waddle more than 320 km across the ice every year to reach their breeding ground.

- **When crossing the ice,** Adélie penguins steer by the sun. They lose their way when the sun goes down.

▶ *The largest penguin at 1.2 m tall, the emperor penguin also weighs in as the heaviest seabird. Each male holds his partner's single egg on his feet for some 60 days until the chick hatches.*

... **FASCINATING FACT** ...
The male emperor penguin keeps the female's egg warm on his feet until it hatches.

117

Sparrows

- **More than 70%** of all bird species – over 5,000 species altogether – are perching birds, or Passerines. They have feet with three toes pointing forwards and one backwards, to help them cling to a perch.

- **Perching birds build** neat, small, cup-shaped nests.

- **Perching birds sing** – this means that their call is not a single sound, but a sequence of musical notes.

  - **Songbirds**, such as thrushes, warblers and nightingales, are perching birds with especially attractive songs.

    - Usually only male songbirds sing – and mainly in the mating season, to warn off rivals and attract females.

◀ *Sparrows are small perching birds found in many parts of the world. Sparrows are seed-eaters with the house sparrow specializing in grain. Changes in farming practices are thought to account for this bird's dramatic decline in numbers in Britain.*

▲ *Starlings often gather on overhead cables ready to migrate.*

- **Sparrows are small**, plump birds, whose chirruping song is familiar almost everywhere.

- **Starlings** are very common perching birds which often gather in huge flocks, either to feed or to roost.

- **All the millions** of European starlings in North America are descended from 100 set free in New York's Central Park in the 1890s.

- **Many perching birds**, including mynahs, are talented mimics. The lyre bird of southeastern Australia can imitate car sirens and chainsaws, as well as other birds.

- **The red-billed quelea** of Africa is the world's most abundant bird. There are over 1.5 billion of them.

119

Birds' eggs and nests

◀ *After they lay their eggs, most birds sit on them to keep their eggs warm until they are ready to hatch. This is called incubating the eggs.*

- **All birds** begin life as eggs. Each species' egg is a slightly different colour.

- **The plover's egg** is pear-shaped. The owl's is round.

- **Hornbills** lay just one egg a year. Partridges lay up to 20 eggs. Hens and some ducks can lay around 350 a year.

- **Most birds build nests** to lay their eggs in – usually bowl-shaped and made from twigs, grasses and leaves.

- **The biggest nest** is that of the Australian mallee fowl, which builds a mound of soil 5 m across, with egg-chambers filled with rotting vegetation to keep it warm.

- **The weaverbirds** of Africa and Asia are very sociable. Some work together to weave huge, hanging nests out of straw, with scores of chambers. Each chamber is for a pair of birds and has its own entrance.

- **Ovenbirds** of Central and South America get their name because their nests look like the clay ovens made by local people. Some ovenbirds' nests can be 3 m high.

- **Flamingos** nest on lakes, building mud nests that look like upturned sandcastles poking out of the water. They lay one or two eggs on top.

- **The great treeswift** lays its single egg in a nest the size of an eggcup.

▼ *The bittern, famous for its bull-like booming call, feeds on animals living in reed beds. This is where it makes its nest.*

.....FASCINATING FACT.....
Great auks' eggs are pointed at one end to stop them rolling off their cliff-edge nests.

121

What are mammals?

- **Mammals** are animals with furry bodies, warm blood, and a unique habit of suckling their young on milk from the mother's teats.

- **Humans and most other mammals** keep their body temperatures at around 37°C, although the three-toed sloth's temperature varies from 24.4°C to 40°C.

- **Fur and fat** protect mammals from the cold. When they do get cold, they curl up, seek shelter or shiver.

- **All mammals** except monotremes (see strange mammals) give birth to live young.

- **Most mammals** are placental – their young are nourished inside the mother's womb through an organ called the placenta until they are fully developed.

- **Marsupials** (see kangaroos and koalas) are not placental. Their young develop mainly in the mother's pouch.

◀ *Pigs have 12 or so babies in a litter and 7 pairs of teats.*

▶ *Sloths do everything slowly – even breed and grow. The baby three-toed sloth takes 6 months to develop in the womb, a long time for a mammal this size.*

- **The time from mating to birth** is called the gestation period. In mammals, it varies from 20 days for some mice to 22 months for elephants.
- **Marsupials** have short pregnancies – the opossum's is just 12 days.
- **Mammals** vary in size from the finger-sized Etruscan shrew to the 30 m long blue whale.
- **One of the earliestmammals** was Megazostrodon, a tiny shrew-like creature. It lived along side the dinosaurs 120 million years ago.

Strange mammals

- **The duck-billed platypus** and the echidnas live in Australia and are the only monotremes – mammals that lay eggs.

- **Duck-billed platypuses** are strange in other ways, too. They have a snout shaped like a duck's bill and webbed feet, which is why they are so happy in water.

- **Platypuses hatch** from eggs in a river-bank burrow.

- **Platypus babies** lick the milk that oozes out over the fur of their mother's belly.

- **Echidnas** are also known as spiny anteaters because they are covered in spines and eat ants.

- **After a female echidna** lays her single egg, she keeps it in a pouch on her body until it hatches.

- **The Tasmanian devil** is a small, fierce, Australian marsupial (see kangaroos and koalas). It hunts at night and eats almost any meat, dead or alive.

  - **Tasmanian devils** stuff their victims into their mouth with their front feet.

◀ The duck-billed platypus is one of only three types of egg-laying mammals or monotremes. Its 'duck bill' can sense weak electrical signals in the water made by the moving muscles of its prey.

▼ *The Tasmanian devil may be small, but can be very fierce.*

- **The sugar glider** is a tiny, mouse-like jungle creature which can glide for 45 m between trees.

- **The aardvark** is a strange South African mammal with a long snout and huge claws. It can shovel as fast as a mechanical digger to make a home or find ants.

125

Kangaroos and koalas

▲ *Koalas drink very little water, and their name comes from an Aboriginal word for 'no drink'.*

- **Kangaroos** are big Australian mammals that hop around on their hind (back) legs.

- **A kangaroo's tail** can be over 1.5 m long. It is used for balance when hopping, and to hold the kangaroo up when walking.

- **Red kangaroos** can hop at 55 km/h for short distances.

- **Red kangaroos** can leap 9 m forwards in one huge bound, and jump over fences that are 2 to 3 m high.

- **There are two kinds of kangaroo** – red kangaroos and grey kangaroos. Red kangaroos live in the dry grasslands of central Australia. Grey kangaroos live in the southeast, in woods and grassland.

- **Kangaroos are marsupials** – animals whose babies are born before they are ready to survive in the outside word and so live for a while protected in a pouch on their mother's belly.

- **Koalas** are Australian mammals that look like teddy bears, but which are no relation to any kind of bear.

- **Like kangaroos,** koalas are marsupials. A koala baby spends 6 months in its mother's pouch and another 6 months riding on her back.

- **Koalas** spend 18 hours a day sleeping. The rest of the time they feed on the leaves of eucalyptus trees.

- **Other Australian marsupials** include the wombat, several kinds of wallaby (which look like small kangaroos) and bandicoots (which looks like rats).

▼ *When they are first born, kangaroos are naked and look like tiny jellybabies – just a few centimetres long, with two tiny arms. But straight away they have to haul themselves up through the fur on their mother's belly and into her pouch. Here the baby kangaroo (called a joey) lives and grows for 6 to 8 months, sucking on teats inside the pouch. Only when it is quite large and covered in fur will it pop out of the pouch to live by itself.*

Newborn kangaroo climbing up its mother's belly

Entrance to pouch

Inside the pouch, the baby sucks on its mother's teat

Mother kangaroo's birth canal

Newborn kangaroo

Young kangaroo or 'joey'.

127

Rabbits and rats

- **Mice and rats** belong to a group of 1,800 species of small mammals called rodents. The group also includes squirrels, voles, lemmings beavers, porcupines and guinea pigs.

- **All rodents** have two pairs of razor-sharp front teeth for gnawing nuts and berries, and a set of ridged teeth in their cheeks for chewing.

- **A rodent's front teeth,** called incisors, grow all the time. Only gnawing keeps them the same length.

- **Rats and mice** are by far the most common rodents – they have adapted well to living alongside humans.

- **Brown and black rats** carry germs for diseases such as food poisoning, plague and typhus.

▶ *Rabbits and hares look like rodents but they belong to another group of mammals called lagomorphs or 'leaping shapes'.*

▶ *Rats and mice have long thin tails, pointed noses, beady black eyes and four very sharp front teeth.*

- **Hares** live above ground and escape enemies through sheer speed. Rabbits live in burrows underground.

- **Baby hares** are born above ground, covered in fur and with their eyes open. Rabbits are born naked and blind in burrows.

- **Rabbits breed quickly** – a female can have 20 babies every month during the breeding season, and her babies will have their own families after 6 months.

- **One single rabbit** could have more than 33 million offspring in just 3 years, if they all survived to breed.

- **A single mouse** can produce up to 34 young in one litter.

129

Beavers

◀ *In North America, beavers were once hunted so much that they were almost wiped out. They are protected by law in some places.*

- **Beavers are large rodents** (see rabbits and rats) with flat, paddle-like tails. They live in northern America and northern Eurasia.

- **Beavers live** in rivers, streams and lakes near woodlands and they are good swimmers, using their webbed feet as flippers and their tail as a rudder.

- **A beaver can swim underwater** for almost 1 km, holding its breath all the way.

- **Beavers can chop down** quite large trees with their incredibly strong front teeth, gnawing around the tree in a ring until it finally crashes down.

- **Beavers feed on** bark as well as tree roots and shrubs. They are especially fond of poplars and willows.

130

- **Beavers build dams** across streams from tree branches laid on to a base of mud and stones. Families of beavers often work together on a dam.

- **Beaver dams** are 5 to 30 m long on average, but they can be up to 300 m long.

- **Beavers repair** their dams year after year, and some beaver dams are thought to be centuries old.

- **In the lake** behind the dam, beavers build a shelter called a lodge to live in during winter. Most lodges are like mini-islands made of branches and mud, with only a few underwater tunnels as entrances.

- **Beaver lodges** keep a beaver family so warm that in cold weather steam can often be seen rising from the ventilation hole.

◀ *The beaver is about 1 m long with powerful limbs and strong claws. Well adapted to its lifestyle, it has nostrils and ears that shut automatically underwater and a coat glossy with waterproofing oils.*

Lemurs and lorises

▼ *India and Sri Lanka are home to the slender loris. It eats many insects including caterpillars.*

- **Lemurs** are small furry creatures with long tails and big eyes. They are primates, like monkeys and humans.

- **Lemurs** live only on the islands of Madagascar and Comoros, off the east coast of Africa.

- **Most lemurs** are active at night and live in trees, but the ring-tailed lemur lives mostly on the ground and is active by day.

- **Lemurs** eat fruit, leaves, insects and small birds.

- **The ring-tailed lemur** rubs its rear on trees to leave a scent trail for other lemurs to follow.

- **In the mating season,** ring-tailed lemurs have stink fights for females, rubbing their wrists and tails in stink glands under their arms and rear – then waving them at rivals to drive them off.

- **Lorises and pottos** are furry, big-eyed primates of the forests of Asia and Africa. All are brilliant climbers.

- **Bushbabies** are the acrobats of the loris family. They get their name because their cries sound like a human baby crying.

- **Bushbabies** are nocturnal animals and their big eyes help them see in the dark. Their hearing is so sensitive they have to block their ears to sleep during the day.

▲ *Ring-tailed lemurs get their name from their black-ringed tail which they raise to show where they are.*

- **Tarsiers** of the Philippines are tiny, huge-eyed primates which look like cuddly goblins. They have very long fingers and can turn their heads halfway round to look backwards.

133

Monkeys

- **Monkeys belong** to a group of mammals called primates, along with apes, humans, lemurs and lorises

- **Monkeys live** mostly in trees, and their hands have fingers and their feet have toes for gripping branches. Most monkeys also have tails.

- **There are 150 species** of monkey, and they live in tropical forests in Asia, Africa and the Americas.

- **New World monkeys** (from the Americas) live in trees and often have muscular tails that can grip like a hand. These tails are described as prehensile.

▶ Spider monkeys are found in the jungles of Central and South America. They are notable for their prehensile tails which can grasp branches much like a 'fifth hand'. The tail is a third longer than the body length.

- **New World monkeys** include howler monkeys, spider monkeys, woolly monkeys and capuchins, as well as marmosets, and tamarins such as the golden lion tamarin.

- **Old World monkeys** (from Africa and Asia) live on grasslands as well as in forests. They include baboons, colobus monkeys, langurs and macaques.

- **Old World monkeys** do not have a prehensile tail, but their thumbs and fingers can point together, like ours can, so they can grasp things well.

- **The proboscis monkey** gets its name from its huge nose (proboscis is another word for nose).

- **Most monkeys** eat anything from fruit to birds' eggs, but baboons may also catch and eat baby antelopes.

▶ *Baboons such as the Hamadryas (sacred) baboon are large, dog-like monkeys which are well adapted to living on the ground in African bush country*

....FASCINATING FACT....
Howler monkeys can howl so loudly
they can be heard over 3 km away.

135

Gorillas and other apes

▲ *Gorillas climb trees only to sleep at night or to pull down branches to make a one-night nest on the ground. They usually walk on all fours.*

● **Apes** are our closest relatives in the animal world. The great apes are gorillas, chimpanzees and the orang utan. Gibbons are called lesser apes.

● **Like us,** apes have long arms, and fingers and toes for gripping. They are clever and can use sticks and stones as tools.

● **Gorillas** are the biggest of all the apes, weighing up to 225 kg and standing as tall as 2 m. But they are gentle vegetarians and eat leaves and shoots.

● **There are two gorilla species,** all from Africa – the western and the eastern lowland gorillas and mountain gorillas.

● **Mountain gorillas** live in the mountains of Rwanda and Uganda. There are only about 650 of them.

● **When danger threatens a gorilla troop,** the leading adult male stands upright, pounds his hands against his chest, and bellows loudly.

● **Chimpanzees** are an ape species that live in the forests of central Africa.

● **Chimpanzees** are very clever and use tools more than any other animal apart from humans – they use leaves as sponges for soaking up water to drink, for example, and they crack nuts with stones.

- **Chimpanzees** communicate with each other through a huge range of grunts and screams. They also communicate by facial expressions and hand gestures, just as humans do. Experiments have shown that they can learn to respond to many words.

- **Only a few orang-utans** remain in the forests of Borneo and Sumatra. They get their name from a local word for 'old man of the woods'.

Gorillas have no hair on their face or chest, and their palms and soles are also bare

▼ *Gorillas live in troops (groups) of a dozen or so. They travel through the forests searching for food led by a mature male, called a silverback because of the silver hairs on his back. Gorillas like to groom each other and cuddle when they rest in the afternoon.*

An adult male has a crest of hair on his head

Baby gorillas are carried by their mother until they are 3 years old

137

Bats

- **Bats** are the only flying mammals. Their wings are made of leathery skin.

- **Most bats sleep** during the day, hanging upside down in caves, attics and other dark places. They come out at night to hunt.

- **Bats find things** in the dark by giving out a series of high-pitched clicks – the bats tell where they are and locate (find) prey from the echoes (sounds that bounce back to them). This is called echo location.

- **Bats are not blind** – their eyesight is as good as that of most humans.

- **There are 900 species** of bat, living on all continents except Antarctica.

- **Most bats feed** on insects, but fruit bats feed on fruit.

▲ *There are about 130 species of fruit bat known as flying foxes. They fly on leathery wings that can span as much as 1.8 m, to feed on fruits as bananas and figs.*

- **Many tropical flowers** rely on fruit bats to spread their pollen.

- **Frog-eating bats** can tell edible frogs from poisonous ones by the frogs' mating calls.

- **The vampire bats** of tropical Latin America feed on blood, sucking it from animals such as cattle and horses. A colony of 100 vampire bats can feed from the blood of 25 cows or 14,000 chickens in one night.

- **False vampire bats** are bats that do not suck on blood, but feed on other small creatures such as bats and rats. The greater false vampire bat of Southeast Asia is one of the biggest of all bats.

▶ *Bats spend their lives in darkness, finding their way with sounds so high-pitched only a young child can hear them.*

Dogs and wolves

▼ *Across Europe and North America the adaptable, clever red fox has taken to living in towns and even cities. It will raid dustbins for food.*

● **The dog family** is a large group of four-legged, long-nosed, meat-eating animals. It includes dogs, wolves, foxes, jackals and coyotes.

● **All kinds of dog** have long canine teeth for piercing and tearing their prey. (Canine means 'dog').

● **When hunting**, dogs rely mainly on their good sense of smell and acute hearing.

● **Wolves** are the largest wild dogs. They hunt together in packs to track down animals bigger than themselves, such as moose, deer, caribou and musk oxen.

● **A wolf pack** may have 7 to 20 wolves, led by the eldest male and female.

● **A wolf pack's territory** may be 1,000 square km or more. Wolves can travel vast distances when hunting.

● **Wolves once lived** all over Europe and North America, but are now rare in Europe and are found only in remote areas of North America as well as Asia.

● **Foxes** are cunning hunters which prowl at night, alone or in pairs. Typical prey includes rats, mice and rabbits.

● **The red fox** has adapted to the growth of towns and cities and may often be seen at night raiding surburban rubbish bins and dumps.

● **The jackals** of Africa look like small wolves, but they hunt alone for small prey and only meet in packs to grab the leftovers from the kill of a lion.

▶ *Most wolves are grey wolves – either the timber wolf of cold forest regions, or the tundra wolf of the Arctic plains.*

Bears

- **Although bears** are the largest meat-eating land animals, they also eat many other foods, including fruits, nuts and leaves.

- **The biggest bear** is the Alaskan brown bear, which grows to 2.7 m long and weighs up to 770 kg.

- **There are 7 species of bear.** Most live north of the equator, in all kinds of environments. Two live south of the equator – the spectacled bear in South America and the sun bear in Southeast Asia.

- **Bears do not hug** their prey to death, as is sometimes thought. Instead, they kill their victims with a powerful cuff from their front paws, or with their teeth.

◀ *The Asian black bear has a jet-black coat of soft, silky fur with white markings on its chest. It also has larger, more rounded ears than other bears. It is an agile climber and often clambers into the branches to rest. This bear eats mostly fruit, nuts, shoots, grubs and insects.*

▶ *The polar bear has a white coat to camouflage it against the Arctic snow when it is hunting seals. Sometimes, only its black nose gives it away.*

- **The grizzly bear** is actually a brown bear with white fur on its shoulders. Grizzly bears from Alaska are the biggest brown bears, along with kodiak bears.

- **Polar bears mainly eat** seals and they are the only truly carnivorous bears.

- **Polar bears catch seals** when the seals poke their heads up through breathing holes in the Arctic ice.

- **Polar bears often swim underwater** and come up under an ice floe to tip seals off. They may also chuck huge chunks of ice at seals to stun them.

- **The sun bear** of Southeast Asia is the smallest bear.

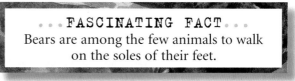

. . . .FASCINATING FACT. . . .
Bears are among the few animals to walk
on the soles of their feet.

Pandas

- **Giant pandas** are large, black-and-white, furry mammals that live in the bamboo forests of western China and Tibet. Most pandas live between 1,500 and 3,000 m above sea level in the moist bamboo forests of western Szechuan and eastern Sikang.

- **Giant pandas are among the rarest species** of animal in the world. There are probably fewer than 1,000 left. The giant panda's habitat has been cut back by the loss of forests for wood and farmland.

- **One reason** that giant pandas are rare is because they feed only on the shoots of bamboos. Some bamboos flower once every century and then die, and it is many years before the seeds grow into new plants.

An extra thumb helps pandas hold the bamboo while they are chewing.

Giant pandas eat only certain kinds of bamboo.

▶ *Giant pandas are big, chubby animals, usually weighing well over 100 kg. When they stand on their hind legs they are as tall as a man. But pandas have inefficient digestive systems and to sustain their huge bulk they have to eat more continuously than most other animals.*

144

- **Giant pandas** spend most of their time sitting around on the ground eating, but they are surprisingly agile tree climbers.

- **Giant pandas spend 12 hours** a day feeding on bamboo shoots, because their digestive system is so ineffective that they have to eat more than 40 kg of bamboo a day.

- **To help it hold the bamboo**, the panda has an extra 'thumb' – it is not really a thumb, but a bone on the wrist which is covered by a fleshy pad.

- **The red panda** is a much smaller animal than the giant panda and it sleeps in trees, curled up like a cat.

- **Red pandas** look a little like raccoons and people once thought that pandas were related to raccoons, even though giant pandas look more like bears. DNA tests have shown that red pandas are close to raccoons, but that giant pandas are closer to bears.

- **In the wild,** giant pandas give birth to one or two cubs a year. The cubs are very tiny and the mother has to give up eating to look after them for the first 10 days. The cubs stay with their mother for nearly one year.

- **Attempts to breed** pandas in zoos have largely failed. Washington Zoo's giant panda Ling Ling, for instance, gave birth to several cubs in the 1970s and 1980s, but the cubs died very soon after birth.

> ... FASCINATING FACT ...
> Chinese zoologists hope to clone giant
> pandas to save them for the future.

Otters

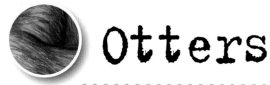

- **Otters** are small hunting mammals which are related to weasels. They are one of the 65 species of mustelid, along with stoats, skunks and badgers.

- **Otters live** close to water and are brilliant swimmers and divers.

- **Otters can close** off their nostrils and ears, allowing them to remain underwater for 4 or 5 minutes.

- **Otters are very playful creatures**, romping around on river banks and sliding down into the water.

- **Otters can use their paws** like hands, to play with things such as stones and shellfish.

- **Otters hunt fish,** mostly at night, but they also eat crayfish and crabs, clams and frogs.

- **Otters usually live** in burrows in riverbanks.

- **Sea otters** live on the shores of western North America.

- **Sea otters will float** on their backs for hours, eating or sleeping. Mother sea otters often carry their baby on their stomachs while floating like this.

▶ *Sea otters rarely come onto land, and seldom venture into water more than 15 m deep. They live along the coasts of the North and West Pacific.*

● **Sea otters eat shellfish.** They will balance a rock on their stomach while
floating on their back, and crack the shellfish by banging it on the rock.

▼ *Freshwater otters use their webbed feet and strong, thick tail to swim speedily
after food. They eat mainly fish but also hunt frogs and water voles.*

Lions

- **Lions** (along with tigers) are the biggest members of the cat family, weighing up to 230 kg. Male lions may be 3 m long.

- **Lions used to live** through much of Europe and Asia. Now they are restricted to East and Southern Africa. Around 200 lions also live in the Gir forest in India.

- **Lions usually live** in grassland or scrub, in families called prides.

- **Lions are hunters** and they prey on antelopes, zebras and even young giraffes. The lionesses (females) do most of the hunting.

- **Male lions** are easily recognizable because of their huge manes. There is usually more than one adult male in each pride and they usually eat before the lionesses and cubs.

- **Lions usually catch** something to eat every four days or so. They can eat up to 40 kg in a single meal. Afterwards they rest for 24 hours.

The mane can be blonde, but gets darker with age

▲ *To other lions, a male lion's shaggy mane makes him look even bigger and stronger, and protects him when fighting. A male lion is born without a mane. It starts growing when he is about two or three and is fully grown by the time he is five.*

- **The lions in a pride** usually spend about 20 hours a day sleeping and resting, and they walk no farther than 10 km or so a day.

- **Lionesses catch their prey** not by speed, but by stealth and strength. They stalk their prey quietly, creeping close to the ground. Then, when it is about 15 m away, the lionesses make a sudden dash and pull the victim down with their strong forepaws.

- **Lionesses usually hunt** at dusk or dawn, but they have very good night vision, and so will often hunt in the dark.

- **Male lion cubs** are driven out of the pride when they are two years old. When a young male is fully grown, he has to fight an older male to join another pride.

◀ *Female lions are called lionesses. They are slightly smaller than males but usually do most of the hunting, often in pairs. There are typically five to ten lionesses in each pride, and each one mates with the male when she is about three years old.*

...**FASCINATING FACT**...
A male lion can drag along a 300 kg zebra
– it would take at least six men to do this.

149

Tigers

- **Tigers** are the largest of the big cats, with huge heads. The average male tiger's body grows to over 2 m long, plus a 1 m-long tail.

- **Tigers live** in the forests of Asia, Sumatra and Java, but as hunters kill them for their skin and farmers clear the forest for land, they are becoming very rare. They now live only on special reserves.

- **Tigers prey on large animals** such as deer, buffalo, antelopes and wild pigs. They hunt silently at night, stalking their prey, then making a sudden bound.

▼ *Tigers are forest dwellers and can climb trees, but most of the time they like to lie around. On hot days, they will often lie in rivers to cool off and, unusually for a cat, they can swim quite well.*

In between the black stripes, the coat is amber or yellow

Most tigers have yellow eyes

Male tigers usually have a ruff of hair around the face

The fur on the throat, belly, and the insides of the legs is whitish

150

- **A tiger is fast and strong** but tires quickly, and it will give up if it fails to catch its prey the first time.

- **Adult tigers** usually live alone, and males try to keep other males out of their territory. But when two tigers meet, they may rub one another's head in greeting.

◄ When a tiger roars, the sound can be heard for 4 or 5 kilometres through the forest.

- **A male tiger's territory** often includes that of two or three females. But they only meet to mate.

- **Tigers mark** out their territory by scratching trees and urinating on them.

- **Usually, two to four cubs** are born at a time. The cubs are playful and boisterous, and are totally dependent on their mother for 2 to 3 years.

- **A tiger's stripes** make it instantly recognizable, but they make good camouflage in long grass and under trees. Each tiger has its own unique pattern of stripes.

- **White tigers** are rare. They have blue eyes, and their stripes are brown and white, not black and gold.

151

Camels

- **Camels** are the biggest desert mammals and they have adapted in many ways to help them live in extremely dry conditions.

- **Arabian camels** have one hump and live mainly in the Sahara desert and the Middle East. Bactrian camels live in central Asia and have two humps.

- **A camel's hump** is made of fat, but the camel's body can break the fat down into food and water when these are scarce.

- **Camels can go** many days or even months without water. But when water is available, they can drink over 200 litres in a day.

◀ *The Bactrian's thick fur helps to keep out the winter cold of the Mongolian high grasslands. The hump of the camel does not store water. It contains fat, which the camel can use as a food store when plants are scarce. However, the fat can be broken down by the camel's special chemistry to produce water too.*

152

▶ *The Arabian camel has been the 'ship of the desert', transporting people and baggage, for thousands of years.*

- **Camels sweat** very little, to save moisture. Instead, their body temperature rises by as much as 6°C when it is hot.

- **The camel's feet** have two joined toes to stop them sinking into soft sand (Arabian camels) or soft snow (Bactrians).

- **The camel's nostrils** can close up completely to block out sand.

- **Camels have** a double row of eyelashes to protect their eyes from sand and sun.

- **The camel's stomach** is huge, with three different sections. Like cows, camels are ruminants – this means they partially digest food, then bring it back into their mouths to chew the cud.

> **...FASCINATING FACT...**
> Camels have by far the worst smelling breath in the entire animal kingdom.

Antelopes and deer

- **Antelopes and deer** are four-legged, hooved animals. Along with cows, hippos and pigs, they belong to the huge group called artiodactyls – animals with an even number of toes on each foot.

- **Antelopes and deer** chew the cud like cows – they chew food again, after first partially digesting it in a special stomach.

- **Most antelope species live** in herds in Africa. Many are very graceful, including the impala and Thompson's gazelle. Most are also fast runners.

- **The horns** on an antelope's head last its lifetime.

▲ *Reindeer cope with harsh winters by finding lichen to eat under the snow – perhaps by smell.*

- **Deer have branching antlers** of bone (not horn) on their heads, which drop off and grow again each year.

- **Most deer species live** in woods and grasslands in mild regions such as northern Europe and North America.

- **The moose or elk** grows antlers more than 2 m wide.

- **Male deer** are called stags, young males are bucks, females are does and babies are fawns.

- **Usually only stags** have antlers. The only female deer to have them are caribou or reindeer, which are the same species of deer but with different names.

▲ *The dik-dik, named after the sound the female makes when alarmed, is a small antelope living in dry scrub in many parts of Africa.*

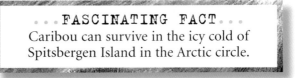

FASCINATING FACT
Caribou can survive in the icy cold of Spitsbergen Island in the Arctic circle.

Giraffes

- **Giraffes** are the tallest mammals, growing to more than 5 m. Their height allows them to reach and eat the leaves, twigs and fruit at the tops of trees.

- **A giraffe's legs** are almost 2 m long.

- **A giraffe's neck** may be over 2 m long, but it only has seven bones – the same number as humans.

- **Giraffes live** in Africa, south of the Sahara, in bush country.

- **The giraffe's long tongue** is so tough that it can wrap around the thorns of a thorn tree to grab twigs.

- **When drinking,** a giraffe has to spread its forelegs wide or kneel down to reach the water. This position makes it very vulnerable to attack by lions.

▲ *Giraffes are the world's tallest animals – but they are five times as light as elephants.*

156

- **When giraffes walk,** they move the two legs on one side of their body, then the two on the other side. Their long legs mean that when it comes to running they can gallop along faster than the speediest racehorse.

- **A giraffe's coat** is patched in brown on cream, and each giraffe has its own unique pattern. The reticulated giraffes of East Africa have triangular patches, but the South African Cape giraffes have blotchy markings.

- **During breeding time**, rival males rub their necks together and swing them from side to side. This is called necking.

- **When first born**, a baby giraffe is very wobbly on its legs and so cannot stand up for at least its first half an hour.

▶ *A close-up of a giraffe's coat. The criss-crossed lines produce a camouflaging effect in the shimmering light of the African grass plains.*

157

Horses

- **Horses** are big, four-legged, hooved animals, now bred mainly for human use.

- **Male horses** are stallions, females are mares, babies are foals, and young males are colts.

- **The only wild horse** is the Przewalski of central Asia.

- **The mustangs** (wild horses) of the USA are descended from tame horses.

- **Tame horses** are of three main kinds – light horses for riding (such as Morgans and Arabs), heavy horses for pulling ploughs and wagons (such as Percherons and Suffolk Punches), and ponies (such as Shetlands).

▶ *All horses, wild and tame, may be descended from the prehistoric Merychippus (see evolution).*

158

▶ *A domestic horse. The rare Przewalski's horse of the Mongolian steppes is probably similar to the ancestor of today's many domestic horse breeds. Horses are built for grazing on grasses and for galloping at high speed for long distances.*

- **Most racehorses and hunting horses** are thoroughbred (pure) Arab horses descended from just three stallions that lived around 1700 – Darley Arabian, Godolphin Barb and Byerly Turk.

- **Lippizaners** are beautiful white horses, the best-known of which are trained to jump and dance at the Spanish Riding School in Vienna.

- **The shire horse** is probably the largest horse, bred after King Henry VIII had all horses under 1.5 m destroyed.

- **You can tell a horse's age** by counting its teeth – a 1-year-old has six pairs, a 5-year-old has twelve.

- **Quarter horses** are agile horses used by cowhands for cutting out (sorting cows from the herd). They got their name from running quarter-mile races.

159

Rhinos and hippos

▶ *The African black rhino is almost extinct in the wild. Between 2 to 3 thousand are left on nature reserves. Some gamekeepers have tried cutting off their horns to make them less of a target for poachers.*

- **Rhinoceroses** are big, tough-skinned animals of Africa and southern Asia.

- **African black and white** rhinos and the smaller Sumatran rhino have two horns in the middle of their heads. Indian and Javan rhinos have just one.

- **Powdered rhino horn** is believed by some to be a love potion, so thousands of rhinos have been slaughtered and most kinds are now an endangered.

- **Baluchitherium** lived 20 million years ago and was a type of the rhino. At over 5 m tall, it was much bigger than any elephant.

- **Hippopotamuses** are big, grey, pig-like creatures that live in Africa. They have the biggest mouth of any land animal.

- **When a hippo yawns** its mouth gapes wide enough to swallow a sheep whole, but it only eats grass.

- **Hippos spend their days** wallowing in rivers and swamps, and only come out at night to feed.

- **A hippo's eyes,** ears and nose are all on the top of its head, and so remain above the water when the rest of its body is completely submerged.

- **The word hippopotamus** comes from the Ancient Greek words for horse (hippo) and river (potamos).

▲ The pygmy hippo is only about 90 cm tall but it is just as tubby as its big cousin and weighs up to 250 kg.

. . .FASCINATING FACT. . .
The African white rhinoceros's horn can grow to over 1.5 m long.

161

Elephants

- **There are three kinds** of elephant – the African forest elephant (Central and West Africa), the African savanna elephant (East and South Africa) and the Asian elephant, which lives in India and Southeast Asia.

- **African elephants** are the largest land animals, growing as tall as 4 m and weighing more than 6,000 kg.

- **Asian elephants** are not as large as African elephants, and have smaller ears and tusks. They also have one 'finger' on the tip of their trunk, while African elephants have two.

- **The scientific word** for an elephant's trunk is a proboscis. It is used like a hand to put food into the elephant's mouth, or to suck up water to squirt into its mouth or over its body to keep cool.

▶ *When the leader of the herd senses danger, she lifts her trunk and sniffs the air – then warns the others by using her trunk to give a loud blast called a trumpet. If an intruder comes too close, she will roll down her trunk, throw back her ears, lower her head and charge at up to 50 km/h.*

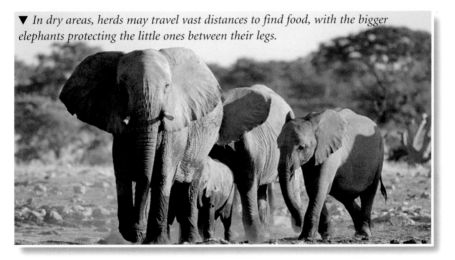

▼ *In dry areas, herds may travel vast distances to find food, with the bigger elephants protecting the little ones between their legs.*

- **Elephants** are very intelligent animals, with the biggest brain of all land animals. They also have very good memories.

- **Female elephants,** called cows, live with their calves and younger bulls (males) in herds of 20 to 30 animals. Older bulls usually live alone.

- **Once a year,** bull elephants go into a state called musth (said 'must'), when male hormones make them very wild and dangerous.

- **Elephants** usually live for about 70 years.

- **When an elephant dies,** its companions seem to mourn and cry.

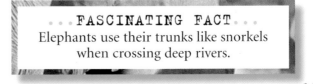

. . . **FASCINATING FACT** . . .
Elephants use their trunks like snorkels
when crossing deep rivers.

163

Farm animals

- **Cattle** are descended from a creature called the wild auroch, which was tamed 9,000 years ago. There are now over 200 breeds of domestic cow.

- **Female cows** reared for milk, butter and cheese production are called dairy cows. They give birth to a calf each year, and after it is born they provide milk twice a day.

- **A typical dairy cow** gives 16 litres of milk a day, or almost 6,000 litres a year.

- **Male cattle** are reared mainly for their meat, called beef. Beef breeds are usually heftier than dairy ones.

▼ *Female cattle are called cows, and males are called bulls. The young are calves. Female calves are also called heifers.*

164

▶ *Domesticated over 4,000 years ago and at first used for religious sacrifices, the chicken now is probably the most numerous bird in the world.*

- **Sheep were first domesticated** over 10,000 years ago. There are now more than 700 million sheep in the world, and 800 different breeds.

- **Hairy sheep** are kept for their milk and meat (lamb and mutton). Woolly sheep are kept for their wool.

- **Hens** lay one or two eggs a day – about 350 a year.

- **To keep hens laying,** their eggs must be taken from them every day. Otherwise the hens will try to nest so they can hatch them.

- **Turkeys** may have got their name from the mistaken idea that they came from Turkey.

...FASCINATING FACT...
When a cow chews the cud, the cud is food regurgitated from one of its four stomachs.

165

Pets

- **There are over 500 breeds** of domestic dog. All are descended from the wolves first tamed 12,000 years ago to help humans hunt. Dogs have kept some wolf-like traits such as guarding territory and hiding bones.

- **Many pet dogs** were originally working dogs. Collies were sheepdogs. Terriers, setters, pointers and retrievers all get their names from their roles as hunting dogs.

- **The heaviest dog breed** is the St Bernard, which weighs over 90 kg. The lightest is the miniature Yorkshire terrier, under 500 g.

- **Cocker spaniels** were named because they were used by hunters to flush out woodcocks in the 14th century.

- **Chihuahuas** were named after a place in Mexico – the Aztecs thought them sacred.

- **The first domestic cats** were wild African bushcats tamed by the Ancient Egyptians to catch mice 3,500 years ago.

- **Like their wild ancestors**, domestic cats are deadly hunters – agile, with sharp eyes and claws – and often catch mice and birds.

▶ *The domestic cat, of which there are over 30 breeds, is a small member of the cat family measuring 75 cm with tail.*

- **Cats spend** a great deal of time sleeping, in short naps, but can be awake and ready for action in an instant.

- **Tabby cats** get their name from Attab in Baghdad (now in Iraq), where striped silk was made in the Middle Ages.

- **A female cat** is called a queen. A group of cats is called a clowder. A female dog is a bitch. A group of dogs is a kennel.

- **All pet golden hamsters** are descended from a single litter which was discovered in Syria in 1930.

▶ *Powerfully built and strong-jawed, pit bull terriers were first bred from bulldogs and terriers as fighting dogs, by miners in the 18th century.*

167

Evolution

- **Charles Darwin's** Theory of Evolution, first published in 1859, showed how all species of plant and animal adapt and develop over millions of years.

- **Darwin's theory** depended on the fact that no two living things are alike.

- **Some animals** start life with characteristics that give them a better chance of surviving to pass the characteristics on to their offspring.

- **Other animals' characteristics** mean that they are less likely to survive.

- **Over many generations** and thousands of years, better-adapted animals and plants survive and flourish, while others die out or find a new home.

- **Fossil discoveries** since Darwin's time have supported his theory, and lines of evolution can be traced for thousands of species.

- **Fossils** also show that evolution is not always as slow and steady as Darwin thought. Some scientists believe change comes in rapid bursts, separated by long slow periods when little changes. Other scientists believe that bursts of rapid change interrupt periods of long steady change.

▼ *One of the horse's earliest ancestors,* Hyracotherium, *appeared about 45 mya. It was a small woodland creature which browsed on leaves. When the woods began to disappear and grasslands became more widespread, it paid to be faster to escape predators. The modern horse,* Equus, *is the latest result of this evolutionary adaptation.*

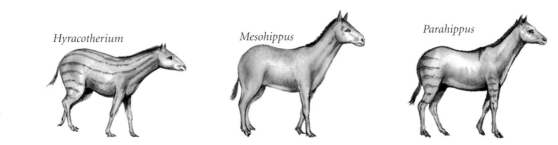

Hyracotherium

Mesohippus

Parahippus

168

- **For the first 3 billion years** of Earth's history, the only life forms were microscopic, single-celled, marine (sea) organisms such as bacteria and amoeba. Sponges and jellyfish, the first multi-celled creatures, appeared by 700 million years ago (mya).

- **About 600 mya,** evolution speeded up dramatically in what is called the Precambrian explosion. Thousands of different organisms appeared within a very short space of time, including the first proper animals with bones and shells.

- **After the Precambrian**, life evolved rapidly. Fish developed, then insects and then, about 380 mya, amphibians – the first large creatures to crawl on land. About 340 mya, reptiles evolved – the first large creatures to live entirely on land.

- **Dinosaurs** developed from these early reptiles about 220 mya and dominated the Earth for 160 million years. Birds also evolved from the reptiles, and cynodonts furry, mammal-like creatures.

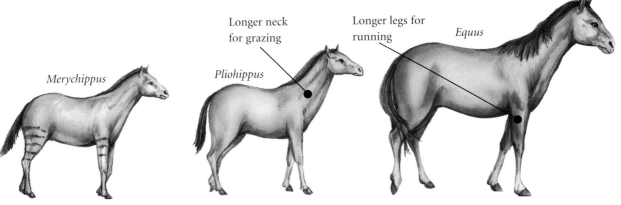

Merychippus

Longer neck
for grazing

Pliohippus

Longer legs for
running

Equus

169

Animal senses

- **Animals** sense the world in a variety of ways, including by sight, hearing, touch, smell and taste. Many animals have senses that humans do not have.

- **Sea creatures** rely on smell and taste, detecting tiny particles drifting in the water. For balance they often rely on simple balance organs called statocysts.

- **Sharks** have a better sense of smell than any other kind of fish. They can detect one part of animal blood in 100 million parts of water.

- **For land animals**, sight is usually the most important sense. Hunting animals often have very sharp eyesight. Eagles, for instance, can see a rabbit moving from as far as 5 km away.

◀ *Hares, like rabbits, have long ears (up to 20 cm long). These are ideal for picking up the faint sounds from approaching predators.*

▶ *The slow loris is nocturnal, and its enormous eyes help it jump safely through forests in the darkness.*

- **Owls** can hear sounds ten times softer than any human can.

- **Male gypsy moths** can smell a mate over 11 km away.

- **Pit vipers** have special sensory pits (holes) on their heads which can pinpoint heat. This lets them track warm-blooded prey such as mice in pitch darkness.

- **The forked tongues** of snakes and lizards are used to taste the air and detect prey.

- **Cats' eyes** absorb 50% more light than human eyes, so they can see very well in the dark.

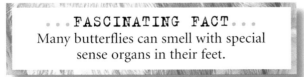

...FASCINATING FACT...
Many butterflies can smell with special
sense organs in their feet.

171

Eating food

◄ The giant anteater is a very odd-looking mammal with its brush-like tail, shaggy fur and long, curved nose. It grows to 2 m long including the tail and shuffles through the wood or scrub in Central and South America, opening nests with its claws and lapping up the ants.

- **Herbivores** are animals that usually eat only plants.

- **Carnivores** are animals that eat animal flesh (meat).

- **Omnivores** eat plants and animals. Many primates such as monkeys, apes and humans are omnivorous.

- **Insectivores** eat insects. Some, such as bats and shrews, have teeth for breaking through insects' shells. Others, such as anteaters, have long, sticky tongues for licking up ants and termites, but few or no teeth.

- **Herbivores** such as cattle, elephants and horses either graze (eat grass) or browse (eat mainly leaves, bark and the buds of bushes and trees).

- **Herbivores** have tough, crowned teeth to cope with their plant food.

- **Carnivores** have pointed canine teeth for tearing meat.

- **Some carnivores,** such as hyenas, do not hunt and instead feed on carrion (the remains of dead animals).

- **Herbivores** eat for much of the time. However, because meat is very nourishing, carnivores eat only occasionally and tend to rest after each meal.
- **Every living thing** is part of a food chain, in which it feeds on the living thing before it in the chain and is in turn eaten by the living thing next to it in the chain.

▲ *Bears are omnivores, eating fish and other meat, although they will eat berries, leaves and almost anything when hungry.*

Defence

- **Animals** have different ways of escaping predators – most mammals run away, while birds take to the air.

- **Some animals** use camouflage to hide (see colours and markings). Many small animals hide in burrows.

- **Turtles and tortoises** hide inside their hard shells.

- **Armadillos** curl up inside their bendy body armour.

- **The spiky-skinned** armadillo lizard of South Africa curls up and stuffs its tail in its mouth.

- **Hedgehogs,** porcupines and echidnas are protected by sharp quills (spines).

- **Skunks** and the stinkpot turtle give off foul smells.

▲ *The nine-banded armadillo is one of 20 species of armadillo. Its armour plating protects it against all but the most determined of predators.*

▼ *Meerkats stand on their hind legs and give a shrill call to alert other meerkats to danger.*

- **Plovers** pretend to be injured to lure hunters away from their young.

- **Many animals defend themselves** by frightening their enemies. Some, such as peacock butterflies, flash big eye-markings. Others, such as porcupine fish and great horned owls, blow themselves up much bigger.

- **Other animals** send out warning signals. Kangaroo rats and rabbits thump their feet. Birds shriek.

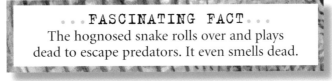

... FASCINATING FACT ...
The hognosed snake rolls over and plays
dead to escape predators. It even smells dead.

Colours and markings

▼ *This red checked nightjar blends superbly with the fallen leaves on which it nests.*

- **Protective colouring** helps an animal hide from its enemies or warns them away.

- **Camouflage** is when an animal is coloured to blend in with its surroundings, making it hard to see.

- **Ground-nesting birds** like the nightjar are mottled brown, making them hard to spot among fallen leaves.

- **The fur of wild pig** and tapir babies is striped and spotted to make them hard to see in dappled jungle light.

- **Squid** can change their colour to blend in with new surroundings.

- **Disruptive colouring** distorts an animal's body so that its real shape is disguised.

- **Bright colours** often warn predators that an animal is poisonous or tastes bad. For example, ladybirds are bright red and the cinnabar moth's caterpillars are black and yellow because they taste nasty.

176

- **Some creatures** mimic the colours of poisonous ones to warn predators off. Harmless hoverflies, for instance, look just like wasps.

- **Some animals** frighten off predators with colouring that makes them look much bigger. Peacock butterflies have big eyespots on their wings.

- **Courting animals,** especially male birds like the peacock, are often brightly coloured to attract mates.

▼ *A zebra's stripes may seem to make it easy to see, but when it is moving they actually blur its outline and confuse predators.*

177

Finding a mate

- **Humans** are among the few animals that mate at any time of year. Most animals come into heat (are ready to mate) only at certain times.

- **Spring** is a common mating time. The warmer weather and longer hours of daylight may trigger the production of sperm in males and eggs in females.

- **Some mammals,** such as bats, bears and deer, have only one mating time a year. Others, such as rabbits, have many.

▼ *A male lion may head a pride of up to 40 individuals. Males regularly have their right to mate with females contested by younger males.*

- **Many large mammals** pair for a short time, but a few (including beavers and wolves) pair for life. Some males (including lions and seals) have lots of mates.

- **To attract a mate,** many animals put on courtship displays such as a special colours, songs and dances.

- **The male capercaillies** (turkey-like birds) of Scotland attract a mate with a clicks and rattles then a pop and a hiss.

- **Great crested grebes** perform dramatic dances in the water and present water plants to one another.

▲ *Prairie dogs live in families called coteries, each made up of a male and several females.*

- **Male bower birds** paint their nests blue with berry juice and line them with blue shells and flowers to attract a mate.

- **Male birds of paradise** flash their bright feathers while strutting and dancing to attract a mate.

- **The male tern** catches a fish as a gift for the female. The male dancefly brings a dead insect which the female eats while mating.

Life on the seashore

- **Seashores** contain a huge variety of creatures which can adapt to the constant change from wet to dry as the tide rolls in and out.

- **Crabs, shellfish** and other creatures of rocky shores have tough shells to protect them from pounding waves and the sun's drying heat.

- **Anemones, starfish** and shellfish such as barnacles have powerful suckers for holding on to rocks.

- **Limpets** are the best rock clingers and can only be prised away if caught by surprise.

- **Anemones** may live on a hermit crab's shell, feeding on its leftovers but protecting it with their stinging tentacles.

- **Rock pools** are water left behind among the rocks as the tide goes out. They get very warm and salty.

- **Rock pool creatures** include shrimps, hermit crabs, anemones and fish such as blennies and gobies.

- **Sandy shores** are home to burrowing creatures such as crabs, razor clams, lugworms, sea cucumbers and burrowing anemones.

- **Sandhoppers** are tiny shelled creatures that live along the tide line, feeding on seaweed.

- **Beadlet anemones** look like blobs of jelly on rocks when the tide is out. But when the water returns, they open a ring of flower-like tentacles to feed.

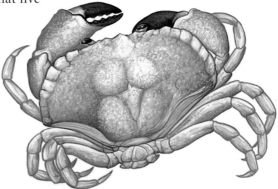

▶ *The edible crab, like all crabs, has five pairs of legs, the front pair with pincers.*

▼ *Crabs, lugworms, sandhoppers, shellfish and many other creatures live on seashores. Many birds come to feed on them.*

Life in the oceans

- **Oceans** cover 70% of the Earth and they are the largest single animal habitat.

- **Scientists divide the ocean** into two main environments – the pelagic (which is the water itself), and the benthic (which is the seabed).

- **Most benthic animals** live in shallow waters around the continents. They include worms, clams, crabs and lobsters, as well as bottom-feeding fish.

- **Scientists call the sunny surface waters** the euphotic zone. This extends down 150 m and it is where billions of plankton (microscopic animals and plants) live.

- **Green plant plankton** (algae) in the oceans produce 30% of the world's vegetable matter each year.

- **Animal plankton** include shrimps and jellyfish.

- **The surface waters** are also home to squid, fish and mammals such as whales.

- **Below the surface zone,** down to about 2,000 m, is the twilight bathyal zone. Here there is too little light for plants to grow, but many hunting fish and squid live.

- **Below 2,000 m** is the dark abyssal zone, where only weird fish like gulper eels and anglerfish live (see strange sea creatures).

- **The Sargasso** is a vast area in the west Atlantic where seaweed grows thick. It is a rich home for barnacles and other sea creatures.

▶ *The tassel-finned anglerfish is hardly larger than your thumb. The fleshy tassels on its chin resemble seaweed.*

▼ *Many kinds of fish and other sea creatures live in the sunlit zone near the surface of the oceans.*

Life in rivers and lakes

- **Rivers, lakes** and other freshwater habitats are home to all sorts of fish, including bream and trout.

- **Fast-flowing streams** are preferred by fish such as trout and grayling. Slow-flowing rivers and lakes are home to tench, rudd and carp.

- **Some fish feed** on floating plant matter, while others take insects from the surface of the water.

- **Common bream and barbel** hunt on the riverbed, eating insect larvae, worms and molluscs.

- **Perch and pike** are predators of lakes and slow-flowing rivers.

- **Pike** are the sharks of the river – deadly hunters that lurk among weeds waiting for unwary fish, or even rats and birds. Pike can weigh as much as 30 kg.

▶ *Upland lakes like these are home to many fish, including char, powan and bullhead. Fish such as brown trout swim in the streams that tumble down into the lake.*

- **Mammals of rivers and lakes** include voles, water rats and otters.
- **Birds of rivers and lakes** include birds that dive for fish (such as kingfishers), small wading birds (such as redshanks, avocets and curlews), large wading birds (such as herons, storks and flamingos), and waterfowl (such as ducks, swans and geese.
- **Insects** include dragonflies and water boatmen.
- **Amphibians** include frogs and newts.

▶ *The grayling looks like a small trout, about 45 cm long, but with a larger sail-shaped back or dorsal fin. Like most members of the salmon family it has little, sharp teeth.*

185

Life on the grasslands

- **Grasslands** form in temperate (moderate temperature) regions where there is too little rainfall for forests, but enough to allow grass to grow.

- **Temperate grasslands** include the prairies of North America, the pampas of South America, the veld of South Africa, and the vast steppes of Eurasia.

- **There is little cover** on grasslands, so many grassland animals have very good eyesight and large ears to detect predators from afar.

- **Some grassland animals escape** from predators by speed. These include jack rabbits, deer, pronghorn antelopes, wild asses and flightless birds like the emu.

- **Some animals,** such as mice and prairie dogs, escape by hiding underground in burrows.

- **Some birds hide** by building their nests in bushes. These include meadowlarks, quails and blackbirds.

- **The main predators** are dogs like the coyote and fox.

- **The North American prairies** have a small wild cat called the bobcat.

▲ *Coyotes eat a vast range of prey from beetles to deer as well as fruits.*

- **Prairie dogs** live in huge underground colonies called towns. One contained 400 million animals and covered over 60,000 square kilometres.

- **When they meet,** prairie dogs kiss each other to find out whether they are from the same group.

186

▲Until they were wiped out by European settlers, vast herds of bison (buffalo) roamed the North American prairies.

Life in woodlands

▲ *On a walk through a deciduous wood, you may be lucky enough to catch a glimpse of a shy young red deer as it crosses a clearing.*

- **Woodlands** in temperate zones between the tropics and the poles are home to many creatures.

- **Deciduous trees** lose their leaves in autumn. Evergreens keep theirs through cold winters.

- **In the leaf litter** under the trees live tiny creatures such as worms, millipedes, and ants and other insects.

- **Spiders, shrews, salamanders and mice** feed on the small creatures in the leaf litter.

- **Some birds**, such as woodcocks, nest on the woodland floor and have mottled plumage to hide themselves.

- **Birds such as owls**, nuthatches, treecreepers, tits, woodpeckers and warblers live on and in trees, as well as insects such as beetles, moths and butterflies, and small mammals such as squirrels and raccoons.

- **Other woodland mammals** include badgers, chipmunks, opossums, stoats, weasels, polecats, pine martens and foxes.

- **Beavers, frogs, muskrats and otters** live near woodland streams.

- **The few large woodland mammals** include bears, deer, wolves and wild boar. Many of these have become rare because woods have been cleared away.

- **In winter,** many birds of deciduous woods migrate south, while small mammals like dormice hibernate.

▶ *The long flight feathers of an owl's wings are tipped with down which muffles the noise of the wing beats. Silent flying allows the owl a much better chance of catching prey.*

189

Life in tropical rainforests

- **Tropical rainforests** are the richest and most diverse of all animal habitats.

- **Most animals** in tropical rainforests live in the canopy (treetops), and are either agile climbers or can fly.

- **Canopy animals** include flying creatures such as bats, birds and insects, and climbers such as monkeys, sloths, lizards and snakes.

- **Many rainforest creatures** can glide through the treetops – these include gliding geckos and other lizards, flying squirrels and even flying frogs.

▶ *Year-round rainfall and warm temperatures make rainforests incredibly lush, with a rich variety of plant life.*

▶ *Like the other 41 species in the bird of paradise group, the king bird lives in rainforests. In courtship the male vibrates his wings for display.*

- **Some tree frogs** live in the cups of rainwater held by plants growing high up in trees.

- **Antelopes, deer, hogs, tapir** and many different kinds of rodent (see ratsand mice) roam the forest floor, hunting for seeds, roots, leaves and fruit.

- **Beside rivers** in Southeast Asian rainforests, there may be rhinoceroses, crocodiles and even elephants.

- **Millions of insect species** live in rainforests, including butterflies, moths, bees, termites and ants. There are also many spiders.

- **Rainforest butterflies and moths** are often big or vividly coloured, including the shimmering blue morpho of Brazil and the birdwing butterflies.

- **Rainforest birds** can be vividly coloured too, and include parrots, toucans and birds of paradise.

191

Life in tropical grasslands

▲ *With their long necks, giraffes can feed on the high branches of the thorn trees that dot the savannah grasslands of Africa.*

- **Tropical grasslands** are home to vast herds of grazing animals such as antelope and buffalo – and to the lions, cheetahs and other big cats that prey on them.

- **There are few places to hide** on the grasslands, so most grassland animals are fast runners with long legs.

- **Pronghorn** can manage 67 km/h for 16 km.

- **There are more than 60 species** of antelope on the grasslands of Africa and southern Asia.

- **A century ago in South Africa,** herds of small antelopes called springboks could be as large as 10 million strong and hundreds of kilometres long.

▼ *The white rhino can weigh over 3.5 tonnes. The 'white' does not refer to the colour, which is pale grey. It means 'wide' from the broad snout.*

- **The springbok** gets its name from its habit of springing 3 m straight up in the air.

- **Grazing animals** are divided into perrisodactyls and artiodactyls, according to how many toes they have.

- **Perrisodactyls** have an odd number of toes on each foot. They include horses, rhinos and tapirs.

- **Artiodactyls** have an even number of toes. They include camels buffaloes, deer, antelope and cattle.

... FASCINATING FACT ...
Cheetahs are the fastest runners in the world, reaching 110 km/h in short bursts.

Life in the desert

- **In the Sahara desert,** a large antelope called the addax survives without waterholes because it gets all its water from its food.

- **Many small animals** cope with the desert heat by resting in burrows or sheltering under stones during the day. They come out to feed only at night.

- **Desert animals** include many insects, spiders, scorpions, lizards and snakes.

- **The dwarf puff adder** hides from the sun by burying itself in the sand until only its eyes show.

- **The fennec fox** and the antelope jack rabbit both lose heat through their ears. This way they keep cool.

- **The kangaroo rats** of California's Death Valley save water by eating their own droppings.

- **The Mojave squirrel** survives through long droughts by sleeping five or six days a week.

- **Swarms of desert locusts** can cover an area as big as 5,000 square kilometres.

- **Sand grouse** fly hundreds of kilometres every night to reach watering holes.

◀ *The fennec fox lives in the Sahara Desert region where it feeds mainly on ants, termites and other tiny prey.*

▼ *Deserts like this are among the world's toughest environments for animals to survive.*

...FASCINATING FACT...
The African fringe-toed lizard dances to keep cool, lifting each foot in turn off the hot sand.

Life in the mountains

● **Mountains** are cold, windy places where only certain animals can survive – including agile hunters such as pumas and snow leopards, and nimble grazers such as mountain goats, yaks, ibex and chamois.

● **The world's highest-living** mammal is the yak, a type of wild cattle which can survive more than 6,000 m up in the Himalayas of Tibet.

● **Mountain goats** have hooves with sharp edges that dig into cracks in the rock, and hollow soles that act like suction pads.

▼ *Sheep like these dall sheep are well equipped for life in the mountains, with their thick woolly coats and nimble feet.*

- **In winter,** the mountain goat's pelage (coat) turns white, making it hard to spot against the snow.
- **The Himalayan snowcock** nests higher than almost any other bird – often above 4,000 m in the Himalayas.
- **The Alpine chough** has been seen flying at 8,200 m up on Everest.
- **Lammergeiers** are the vultures of the African and southern European mountains. They break tough bones, when feeding, by dropping them from a great height on to stones and then eating the marrow.
- **The Andean condor** of the South American Andes is a gigantic scavenger which can carry off deer and sheep. It is said to dive from the skies like a fighter plane (see also vultures).
- **The puma,** or mountain lion, can jump well over 5 m up on to a rock ledge – that is like you jumping into an upstairs window.
- **The snow leopard** of the Himalayan mountains is now one of the rarest of all the big cats, because it has been hunted almost to extinction for its beautiful fur coat.

▶ *The puma ranges from southern canada through North and central America to Patagonia in South America. It has a muscular build and uses the stalk-and-pounce method to catch prey.*

Life in cold regions

- **The world's coldest places** are at the Poles in the Arctic and Antarctic, and high up mountains.

- **Only small animals** such as ice worms and insects can stand the extreme polar cold all year round.

- **Insects** such as springtails can live in temperatures as low as -38°C in Antarctica, because their body fluids contain substances that do not freeze easily.

- **Birds** such as penguins, snow petrels and skuas live in Antarctica. So do the leopard seals that eat penguins.

- **Polar seas** are home to whales, fish and shrimp-like krill.

- **Fish of cold seas** have body fluids that act like car anti-freeze to stop them freezing.

- **Mammals such as polar bears**, sea lions and walruses are so well insulated against the cold with their fur and fat that they can live on the Arctic ice much of the year.

- **Many animals** live on the icy tundra land in the far north of America and Asia. They include caribou, Arctic foxes and hares, and birds such as ptarmigans and snowy owls.

- **Arctic foxes and hares**, ermines and ptarmigans turn white in winter to camouflage them against the snow.

◀ *The leopard seal is so-called because of its spotted grey coat. Its diet includes fish, squid and other seals. It lives on the pack ice around Antarctica.*

▲ *Other animals are the only substantial food in the Arctic wastes, so polar bears have to be carnivorous.*

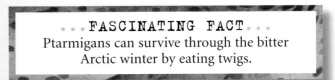

····**FASCINATING FACT**····
Ptarmigans can survive through the bitter
Arctic winter by eating twigs.

199

Baby animals

- **All baby mammals** except monotremes (see strange mammals) are born from their mother's body, but most other creatures hatch from eggs.

- **Most creatures** hatch long after their parents have disappeared. Birds and mammals, though, usually look after their young.

- **Most birds** feed their hungry nestlings until they are big enough to find food themselves.

- **Some small birds** may make 10,000 trips to the nest to feed their young.

- **Cuckoos** lay their egg in the nest of another, smaller bird. The foster parents hatch it and look after it as it grows. It then pushes its smaller, foster brothers and sisters out of the nest.

▶ *Lion cubs are looked after by several females until they are big enough to fend for themselves. Like many babies they have big paws, head and ears for their body.*

- **Mammals nurse** their young (they feed them on the mother's milk). The nursing period varies. It tends to be just a few weeks in small animals like mice, but several years in large animals like elephants.

- **Many animals** play when they are young. Playing helps them develop strength and co-ordination, and practise tasks they will have to do for real when adults.

- **When they are young,** baby opossums cling all over their mother as she moves around.

- **Some baby animals,** including baby shrews and elephants, go around in a long line behind the mother, clinging to the tail of the brother or sister in front.

▶ *A baby elephant is fed by its mother for two years. By the time it is fully grown it will be eating about 150 kg of food each day – the weight of two people!*

201

Communication

- **Crows** use at least 300 different croaks to communicate with each other. But crows from one area cannot understand crows from another one.

- **When two howler monkey troops** meet, the males scream at each other until one troop gives way.

- **The male orang-utan** burps to warn other males to keep away.

- **Dogs** communicate through barks, yelps, whines, growls and howls.

- **Many insects communicate** through the smell of chemicals called pheromones, which are released from special glands.

- **Tropical tree ant species** use ten different pheromones, combining them with different movements to send 50 different kinds of message.

◄ *Orang-utans are shy and seldom seen. However, they may be heard occasionally – making burping noises to scare off other males!*

- **A gorilla** named Coco was trained so that she could use over 1,000 different signs to communicate, each sign meaning different words. She called her pet cat 'Soft good cat cat', and herself 'Fine animal gorilla'.

- **Female glow worms** communicate with males by making a series of flashes.

- **Many birds** are mimics and can imitate a whole variety of different sounds, including the human voice and machines like telephones.

▶ *Lone wolves often howl at dusk or in the night to signal their ownership of a particular territory and to warn off rival wolves.*

....FASCINATING FACT....
Using sign language, Coco the gorilla took an IQ test and got a score of 95.

Surviving the winter

- **Some animals** cope with the cold and lack of food in winter by going into a kind of deep sleep called hibernation.

- **During hibernation**, an animal's body temperature drops and its heart rate and breathing slow, so it needs little energy to survive.

- **Small mammals** such as bats, squirrels, hamsters, hedgehogs and chipmunks hibernate. So do birds such as nighthawks and swifts.

- **Reptiles** such as lizards and snakes go into torpor whenever the temperature gets too low. This is a similar state to hibernation.

- **Butterflies and other insects** go into a kind of suspended animation called diapause in winter.

- **The pika** (a small lagomorph) makes haystacks from grass in summer to provide food for the winter.

▼ *With its bright fur and neat ear tufts, the red squirrel is very distinctive. It sometimes buries seeds and nuts, and sniffs them out later in the year from deep in the soil.*

▶ *Many mammals survive cold winters by hibernating. Some, like this Arctic fox, will sleep for a few days at a time when there is little food to be found.*

- **Beavers** collect branches in autumn and store them next to their lodges so they can feed on the bark during the winter.

- **Bears** go to sleep during winter, but not all scientists agree that they go into true hibernation.

- **Squirrels** bury stores of nuts in autumn to feed on during winter. They seem to have remarkable memories, as they can find most stores when they need them.

. . . **FASCINATING FACT** . . .
Macaque monkeys in Japan keep warm in winter by bathing in hot volcanic springs.

205

Migration

- **Migration** is when animals move from one place to another to avoid the cold or to find food and water.

- **Some migrations** are daily, some are seasonal, and some are permanent.

- **Starlings** migrate every day from the country to their roosts in the city.

- **Many birds, whales seals and bats** migrate closer to the tropics in the autumn to escape the winter cold.

▲ *No other creature migrates so far every year as the Arctic tern. It breeds in the short Arctic summer, then flies halfway around the world to spend another summer in Antarctica.*

- **One knot** (a kind of small bird) took just 8 days to fly 5,600 km, from Britain to West Africa.

- **Barheaded geese** migrate right over the top of the Himalayan mountains, flying as high as 8,000 m.

- **Migrating birds** are often brilliant navigators. Bristle-thighed curlews find their way from Alaska to tiny islands in the Pacific 9,000 km away.

- **Shearwaters,** sparrows and homing pigeons are able to fly home when released by scientists in strange places, thousands of kilometres away.

- **The Arctic tern** is the greatest migrator, flying 30,000 km from the Arctic to the Antarctic and back again each year.

- **Monarch butterflies** migrate 4,000 km every year, from North America to small clumps of trees in Mexico. Remarkably, the migrating butterflies have never made the journey before.

▼ *In summer, moose spend most of the time alone. But in winter they gather and trample areas of snow (called yards) to help each other get at the grass beneath.*

207

Index

Index

Index

Index

Index

Index

Index

Index

Acknowledgements

The publishers would like to thank the following artists
who have contributed to this book:

Lisa Alderson, Martin Camm, Jim Channell, Richard Draper,
Rob Jakeway, Steve Kirk, Mick Loates, Alan Male,
Terry Riley, Mike Saunders, Sarah Smith

The publishers would like to thank Ted Smart
for the generous loan of his illustrations.

All pictures from the Miles Kelly Archives